Fighting
FEAR
with
FAITH

This is a very interesting, well-written book that will become a very useful instrument for anyone trying to advise those who are fearful, whether this is on a one-to-one basis or in a group.

The chapters comprehensively deal with almost every kind of fear, while skillfully applying well-suited texts. Two different types of Bible studies based on the earlier text are included.

The author's main aim is to distinguish between healthy and non-healthy fears. Although it is directed mainly at women, it could also have a much wider use. A striking quote by Oswald Chambers that depicts something of the tenor of this book is as follows:

The remarkable thing is when you fear God you fear nothing, whereas if you do not fear God you fear everything else.

Mairi Harman

Mother of 5, grandmother of 13 who enjoys assisting her husband in his ministry
Ocean Grove, Australia

Fear can be both healthy and unhealthy and both aspects are dealt with great understanding in the book. It is not a subject about which many people speak or are open.

Being an alcoholic, my own life was full of fears and terrors from which I escaped through a bottle. Becoming a Christian didn't take my fears away and I had all sorts of fears such as sleeping in the dark, going back to the drink and having a fear about living and of what each day would bring.

Through meditating on Scripture such as 'perfect love drives out fear' and 'I didn't give you a spirit of fear but of love, power and a sound mind', I was able to overcome these fears and put it into practice by having faith to put the light off to sleep in the dark. Today I live my life not by fear but by faith.

I don't think the subject of 'fear' is one that is explored enough in our Christian walk and I haven't heard many sermons on the subject either. This book would be an excellent study book because fear is such a strong emotion and affects every person in life at some point or other. I will certainly be using it in our own study group and would recommend it to others.

May Nicholson

Founder of Preshal Trust, Glasgow, Scotland
Her story is told in *Miracles from Mayhem*

DENISE GEORGE

FIGHTING
FEAR
WITH
FAITH

Weathering the Storms
with God's Promises

CHRISTIAN
FOCUS

Copyright © Denise George 2011

paperback ISBN 978-1-84550-716-9
ePub ISBN 978-1-84550-995-8
Mobi ISBN 978-1-84550-794-7

10 9 8 7 6 5 4 3 2 1

Previously published in 2005 under the title *Weathering the Storms.*

Reprinted in 2011 and 2013
by
Christian Focus Publications,
Geanies House, Fearn,
Ross-shire, IV20 1TW, Scotland, United Kingdom
www.christianfocus.com

Cover design
by
DUFI-ART.com

Printed by
Bell and Bain, Glasgow

CONTENTS

DEDICATION

For Dr Calvin Miller and Barbara Miller—my *forever* friends.

Foreword

Green, blue, yellow, orange, and red. There was a time when these everyday colors only brought to mind the simple pleasures of life—a box of crayons, the arched rainbow overhead, or an array of flowers in our garden. Today, however, they represent the level of our fears. I saw the color-coded chart as I passed through airport security, an unwelcome reminder of the current threat of terrorist activity. In a world with plenty of reasons for fear, this new fear has managed to insert itself into our post-9/11 lives with such importance we have color-coded it.

The first time I met Denise George, I was impressed by her Southern warmth that quickly put others at ease, her heart for ministry to women, and her determination to do something about the hurts that distress and hold us captive. In this book, she puts fear on the table, a problem that daily touches us all in deeply private and unnervingly public ways.

9

As a wife, mother, and frequent flyer, I'll admit I am no stranger to fear. I've suffered my share of sleepless nights, when fear and anxiety have had a stronger grip on me than my exhaustion. I hardly slept a wink the night before my husband's heart catheterization. Sometimes I wonder if my stomach will ever stop turning into knots over my daughter and the choices, challenges, and temptations confronting her. As a traveler, I've felt a surge of distrust and fright over a suspicious looking fellow passenger. No matter how often I fly, my palms still turn moist the instant the plane encounters more than the usual turbulence in flight, even though I look like I'm calmly reading a book. Living in a broken, fallen world, our fears remind us that we are not in control and the stakes are high, for the uncertainties and dangers that surround us threaten our well-being and happiness and that of our loved ones.

In this book, Denise George invites us to bring our fears—both real and imagined—to the only one who truly is in control, the God who calls us to "fear not". She doesn't write from an ivory tower, but joins us as a friend and fellow struggler against this ever-present foe. Every reader will find her own fears in the topics Denise discusses. I appreciate her honest refusal to sidestep the very real possibility that the things we most fear may actually come to pass. She doesn't urge us to summon up a triumphant Christian bravery. Instead, she calls us to face our fears under the gaze of God, who calls us to trust him with all of the uncertainties and anxieties of our lives. According to Denise, even our fears are purposeful, for they expose our need for God and drive us to him. She gently points the way for us to move from fear to faith, by setting God, and his unchanging promises, before us.

Whatever the color of your fear, this book offers balm for your soul. Read and ponder it, then share it with a friend!

Carolyn Custis James
Author of *When Life And Beliefs Collide: How Knowing God Makes a Difference; The Gospel of Ruth: Loving God Enough to Break the Rules; Lost Women of the Bible: The Women We Thought We Knew; Understanding Purpose*; and *Half the Church: Recapturing God's Global Vision for Women.* Based on:

"I am the vine; you are the branches. If you remain in me and I in you, you will bear much fruit; apart from me you can do nothing.... This is to my Father's glory, that you bear much fruit, showing yourselves to be my disciples." (Jesus in John 15:5, 8)

Introduction

I learned about survival in a garden. As a little girl, I played beneath the stately elm trees that overshadowed my grandmother's gardens. They looked like huge umbrellas opened up to the sky. As I grew, the elms grew, tall and strong.

My grandmother's elms canopied her small, white-gabled farm house in Rossville, Georgia. "Mama" (pronounced "MAW-maw") told me her great great-pioneer grandparents made wagon wheel hubs, fence posts, and furniture from elm trees.

"Elm wood's tough," she said. "Doesn't easily split."

She said Indians (Native Americans), who once lived on this same soil, made ropes from elm bark.

As a child, I rocked my baby dolls to sleep under those graceful, arching beauties that shaded me from summer's hot Southern sun. I climbed their sturdy branches and peeked into orioles' nests. I swung from tire-swings strapped to their limbs. I searched for Easter eggs around their thick bases. And many times, as a romantic budding teen, I leaned against an elm and dreamed the dreams that young girls dream.

Mama said the elm's roots grow as deep into the ground as their branches grow high into the sky. Her roots dig deep, she said, and send food, water, and air through the trunk to the branches. Strong roots anchor the elm, hold her up straight, and help her stand up to storms. Without her roots, she told me, elms would die. They're her means of survival, her lifeline.

As I grew older, I didn't think much about elms. Time no longer allowed climbing trees and swinging on tires. School, marriage, travels, and babies filled my waking hours. Not until the morning of April 19, 1995, did I stop and ponder the true majesty and strength of the American elm.

That morning, a young man filled with hate, Timothy McVeigh, set off a homemade bomb that exploded in front of the Alfred P. Murrah Federal Building in Oklahoma City. The explosion killed 168 people, nineteen of them children. It leveled most of the building, set nearby cars ablaze, and devastated the grounds.

After the smoke cleared, only one thing remained standing in the rubble: a seventy-five-year-old American elm tree. Deep-rooted and strong trunked, it had sustained the blast's full force and survived. When I visited the Oklahoma City National Memorial site several years later, I saw they had named it: "Survivor Tree."

I've met many Christian women who, like the elm tree, are so securely joined to the Lord, whose roots grow so deep in God's Word, who stand so strong on God's promises, they too can survive life's unexpected blasts. They too are deeply anchored and grounded in Scripture's sturdy foundation, and dread no danger from life's inevitable storms. But I've met many others who live in constant fear—immobilized and/or devastated by hard times.

Maybe you've picked up this book because you are dealing with some unhealthy fears, and yearn to find freedom from them. Or maybe your mother, daughter, daughter-in-law, or another loved one is dealing with unhealthy fear, and you need the tools to help her. Throughout the following pages, you'll learn a lot about fear. You'll discover how to differentiate between healthy fears (those that are God's gift to encourage you) and unhealthy fears (those that are Satan's tool to discourage you). You need not live your life in the grip of unhealthy fear. Through God's promises and Christ's examples, you can conquer your unhealthy fears, and you can find freedom from them.

Did you know that the opposite of fear is not courage? Most people believe that, but it's not true. The opposite of fear is faith. As your roots deepen in God's Word, and as He helps you identify and analyze unhealthy fears, these fears will begin to fade. Strong, deep roots, steadily growing in faith, will equip you to weather all life's storms. You'll not only survive, and rid your life of unhealthy fear, but you'll thrive in your faith and love for God. My prayer for you is that, through the guidance of these pages that point you to the wisdom of God's Word, you'll find release from unhealthy fear's bondage – so that God can use you fully, and unhindered, in His remarkable ministry.

Now, let's begin our journey!

Denise George
Spring 2011

SECTION 1

WHAT WOMEN FEAR

1

Fear – A Strong Human Emotion

The oldest and strongest emotion of [humankind] is fear.

H. P. Lovecraft

Before we begin, let's look at those things that women might fear. Know that every woman wrestles at some time in her life with fear. (Of course, so do men. But I'm writing this book primarily for women.) This past Christmas, (2009), my husband, Timothy, and I took our two grown children – my daughter, Alyce, and my son, Christian, and his wife, Rebecca, to Italy for the holidays. We had a remarkable trip, walking in the footsteps of St. Francis in Assisi, eating Italian pasta together around a big dinner table in Rome, strolling the streets and shops of Sorrento, touring the ruins of Herculaneum. But on Christmas night, when I called the States to check on my mother, I learned about the "Christmas Bomber" incident.

On Northwest Airlines Flight 253, a Nigerian man, Umar Farouk Abdulmutallab, working with al-Qaeda in Yemen, came close to blowing up a plane in flight with 290 passengers aboard. The plane was flying from Amsterdam to

Detroit, Michigan. Officials found more than eighty grams of PETN powder (an explosive related to nitro-glycerin), as well as a liquid-filled syringe, sewn in the twenty-three-year-old student's underwear. When Abdulmutallab combined the powder and liquid, shortly before landing in Detroit, he created a flash bomb. Passengers and air crew jumped Abdulmutallab and extinguished the blaze before it could damage the plane. Fortunately, the Christmas Day bombing was botched, and the 290 people aboard the flight lived to see Detroit's airport.

We had scheduled our own flights from Italy back to the United States for New Year's Day. If a young Nigerian could board an international flight headed to the States with undetected explosives in his underwear, why couldn't an al-Qaeda agent in Rome, Italy, do the same thing? How safe were we flying home only a week after the near bombing incident?

Fear. Security tightened at the Rome airport, and we were patted down, searched, and questioned before and after the flight. We spent twelve long hours flying over the Atlantic Ocean, and wondering if we, too, might be in danger from an explosive-packing passenger in the next seat. When we landed in Atlanta, Georgia, we were again patted down, searched, and questioned before we could leave the airport.

Surely, many women today live in a constant state of fear. Former newspaper advice columnist Ann Landers received an average of 10,000 letters a month from people (mostly women) burdened with life's problems. When asked what problem most people struggle with, she replied quickly: "Fear!"[1]

---

1   Gospel Communication Network, Online Christian Resources, July 29, 1996.

The dictionary defines "fear" as a "sudden attack, anxiety, or agitation caused by the presence or nearness of danger, evil, or pain."

As society changes, people's fears also change. For instance, researchers at Johns Hopkins University reported that thirty years ago, the greatest fears of grade school children were: 1) Animals, 2) Being in a dark room, 3) High places, 4) Strangers, 5) Loud noises. Today, kids are afraid of the following: 1) Divorce, 2) Nuclear war, 3) Cancer, 4) Pollution, 5) Being mugged.[2] In 2005, A Gallup Poll was conducted to reveal the most common fears of teenagers in the United States. The top ten list goes like this:

Terrorist attacks
Spiders
Death
Failure
War
Heights
Crime/Violence
Being alone
The future
Nuclear war

Other common fears include public speaking, going to the dentist, pain, cancer and snakes. Most of these basic fears are carried into adulthood. Many women today fear these same things.[3]

Most women I've talked with fear those things that are stronger than they are, things they cannot control,

---

2   *Back to the Bible Today*, Summer, 1990, p. 5. Found at: http://www.sermonillustrations.com/a-z/f/fear.htm. Accessed: January 20, 2010.

3   Found at: http://health.howstuffworks.com/human-nature/emotions/other/fear5.htm. Accessed: January 20, 2010.

things that threaten their own lives and the lives of those they love. They fear a force that goes out of control—like cancer and crime and hurricanes, and plane-bombers—the epitome of chaos. Chaos poses a threat to life. It is mysterious, and often attacks without warning. We don't understand why cancer cells go berserk, and malignancy invades a body. We don't understand why some people wreak havoc on others, committing crimes that hurt and violate. Why does a young, healthy student want to blow up an airplane, killing passengers and himself? It makes no sense. We don't understand why hurricanes devastate homes, kill families, and inflict bankrupting damage. Recently, Hurricane Katrina and her chaotic winds and waters almost sent New Orleans to her grave. She proved an out-of-control and deadly incident. These kinds of events cause terror and chaos.

Chaos means the "system has turned against itself: The cancer is one of our own cells gone wild; the criminal is a fellow human being with malignant intention"; the hurricane is "mother nature" turned fierce, no longer nurturing, but destroying.[4]

Consider what happened the day after Christmas 2003, at 5:27 a.m. A violent earthquake opened the ground and flattened the historical city of Bam, Iran. For days, survivors beat their chests, screamed, and cried. In their search for loved ones, they dug through rubble until their bare hands bled. In the freezing cold temperatures, and without food or water, they hunted for missing parents, husbands, wives, and children. The unexpected earthquake brought death to tens of thousands, and injury and terror to thousands more.[5]

4   Morton Bard and Dawn Sangrey, *The Crime Victim's Book* (New York, N.Y.: Basic Books, Inc., 1979), p. 25.

5   CNN.com, "Thousands Feared Dead in Iran Quake," 26 December 2003, online.

And who will ever forget the sudden tsunami that hit western Indonesia the day after Christmas 2004, killing nearly 300,000 people in nearly a dozen countries?

Nature's fury is frightening. She cannot be controlled. Monitored, probed, examined, studied—but not controlled. Nature's terrifying calamities can come quickly, unexpectedly, and they can change the course of our lives.

Fear of Nature's unexpected chaos is nothing new. In 79 A.D., only a few years after the Apostle Paul died in Rome, Mount Vesuvius erupted, sending nine feet of volcanic ash onto the cities of Pompeii and Herculaneum on the coast of Southern Italy. The chaos lasted nineteen hours, and buried the cities and their residents.

"You could hear women lamenting, children crying, men shouting," writes eyewitness Pliny the Younger. "There were some so afraid of death that they prayed for death. Many raised their hands to the gods, and even more believed that there were no gods any longer and that this was one unending night for the world."[6]

The cities stayed buried for nearly 1700 years. When discovered and the volcanic ash removed, they became a "time capsule" of life in 79 A.D.

In Sorrento, Italy, our hotel sat on the rocky coast right beneath Mount Vesuvius. Experts have predicted Vesuvius is long overdue for its next eruption. I must admit, I had a few unsettling moments as I lay in bed at night and wondered about this "overdue eruption."

Surely, Nature cannot be controlled—not in 79 A.D. or in 2010 A.D., and can still bring gnawing fear to the pit of our stomachs. It's so true – we most fear what we cannot control.

---

6   Found at: http://dsc.discovery.com/convergence/pompeii/history/
     history.html. Accessed: January 20, 2010..

One day, less than a half-century before Mount Vesuvius blew her top, a wicked storm engulfed a tiny boat on Lake Galilee. I've sailed on Lake Galilee in a wooden boat, and I know firsthand that storms can stir up quickly and unexpectedly. On that day long ago, in the boat's bow lay Jesus. Sound asleep. Probably snoring. Exhausted from teaching, preaching, and healing. The frightened disciples, who sailed with him, clung to the boat and feared for their lives. They became like timid toddlers, terrified of tipping, sinking, and drowning. Surely, it was a legitimate fear. Had I been there, I might have asked:

"James, Peter, John, and you others frightened and scared—how can you fear the squall when Jesus, himself, floats in your boat?"

"Why do you scream, 'Master, Master, we're going to drown?!' Why do you hold so tight to the helm when right beside you is Jesus' hand?"

"Jesus, open your sleepy eyes, raise your head, calm the winds and waves that wildly whip at your disciples' backs. Stand up, point your finger at the chaos, and shout: 'Stop that right now, winds and waves!' Then Jesus, lie back down and go to sleep. Erase the disgust that covers your face, as you ask your disciples: 'Men, where's your faith'?"

Jesus didn't say: "Men, where's your courage!" But instead, he asked: "Men, where's your faith?"

"Jesus, sleep once more, snore, and ignore your disciples' angst as they stare in shock and ask each other: 'Who is this? He commands even the winds and the water, and they obey him.'" (See Luke 8:22-5.)

On another dark night, frightened disciples furiously row their fragile boat against a rough Lake Galilee storm. This time, however, Jesus isn't with them in the boat. They are more than three miles from Galilee's shore. They paddle and panic, and fear death by drowning.

They almost give up hope, almost give in to the winds and waves, when they see something on the water that scares them far worse than the storm's fury. A strange shadowy figure stands on the water's surface and walks toward them. They are terrified. Then the "shadow" speaks: "It is I; don't be afraid." Feelings of panic stop. Blood pressures lower. Hearts beat normally again. The frightened disciples welcome Jesus into the boat and row back to shore. (See John 6:16-21.)

All human beings—even those closest to the physical body of Jesus, Himself—have felt terrifying fear. Fear is a God-planted, human emotion. And it has a purpose.

Are you facing a storm in your life right now? Are you afraid you might not survive it? Are you rowing your boat against wicked weather with no hope for rescue in sight? Is a past storm proving stronger than you are, out of control, and interfering with your life?

Storms can sink us in various ways. What present storm do you face? What past storm has rendered you inept? Sudden illness? Possible surgery? Job loss? Financial agony? A broken relationship? A husband's heart attack? A mother's death? A loved one's addiction?

Has your past or present storm come to you in life-shattering words—

From your husband: "I don't love you anymore. I want a divorce."

From your teenaged son: "I'm homosexual, and I have HIV."

From your abusive spouse: "If you call the police, I'll kill you!"

From your local police: "We can't arrest the stalker until he hurts your daughter."

From your eldest son: "I am being shipped to Iraq for active duty."

From your grandson's school principal: "Your grandson's been arrested on drug possession."

What is your own particular storm right now? Does it threaten to knock you off your feet, rear-end your plans, dash your family's dreams, or destroy your future? You may wonder if you can survive its impact and devastation. Throughout the pages of this book, we will look at our fears—both past and present—and discover how we can stand boldly, courageously, and faithfully in their midst.

Remember: The opposite of fear is not courage, but faith. When Jesus' disciples panicked in the storm, Jesus asked them: "Where is your faith?" Courage is what happens when you employ your faith. But faith—those strong roots that reach deep into the foundation of God and his Word—keep you standing strong and secure and sturdy and stable. No matter what storm hits, you are supported by faith. You need not fear uprooting. Courage is admirable. But faith is necessary. When branches face storms, they stay closely attached to their vine, and they hear the deep-root promises of the One who dearly loves them: "It is I; don't be afraid."

2

The Fear of Death

One thing all people have in common regardless of race, creed, gender, personality tendency, educational or economic status or age is the experience of being afraid.

Wayne and Joshua Mack, *The Fear Factor*

Death—the end of one's earthly existence—proves to be a tremendous fear among women. We fear not only death, but the process of dying, and the pain and suffering that can accompany our death.

Do you fear death? My friend, Glenda, a woman of strong Christian faith, admits she does.

"One of my great fears is how I will die," she confesses. "I want the circumstances surrounding my death to be dignified and honorable to God. But I know I don't have a choice in these matters."

Glenda is right. She cannot control her death any more than she can control the weather.

My friend, Gena, a Christian wife and the mother of six, also fears death.

"I believe I first encountered this fear of death when a church member took ill in choir rehearsal," she told me.

"She was doing great, and singing with all her might. Then she suddenly had a terrible headache, and we rushed her to the hospital. She died shortly after that."

The swiftness of the woman's death stunned Gena.

"After she died, a fear of death came over me, and I couldn't shake it. It became even more pronounced at bedtime. Later it developed into an overwhelming feeling of panic. I couldn't drive at times, and I feared going to sleep because I was afraid I wouldn't wake up."

The fear of death, intensified by feelings of panic, threw a wrench into the cogs of Gena's busy schedule. Her doctor prescribed sleeping pills.

"The pills helped me to sleep," Gena said, "but I suffered side effects. I became temporarily incoherent, and said strange things to my husband and kids."

Gena's fear of death prompted her to seek professional help. With the aid of a Christian counselor, she eventually overcame her fear. The feelings of panic stopped too. Gena resumed her schedule.

Perhaps you, too, fear death. You may wonder: What happens when I die? Will my death be painful? Will I die with dignity? What's on the other side of death? Where will I go? How will I get there? Will the experience be terrifying? Will I cease to be, or will I be alive in another form? Will I have a body? Will I look like myself? Will loved ones, already departed, be there to greet me?

It's no wonder why Don Piper's book, Ninety Minutes in Heaven, written with my friend, Cecile Murphey, has sold nearly six million copies! After a fatal car crash, Piper, pronounced dead by paramedics, lay lifeless in the rain, covered by a tarp, for ninety minutes. During that time, Piper claims he went to heaven. Through the prayers of a passerby, Don Piper regained life and writes about his experiences during his time in heaven. Didn't Piper really die? He claims he did. It's a fascinating book, and it seeks to answer all the many questions most of us have about dying and death and the hereafter.

If your fear of death interferes with your living, let me tell you what God's Word says about death.

God tells us we won't face death alone, but with Jesus.

God promises us that, as believers in Jesus Christ, we'll have a place in his heavenly mansion.

God assures us of eternal life with him.

Jesus, after his earthly life, faced death. He has experienced dying and death. And he came back to reassure us in our fears of death.

Sometimes, however, we wonder if we can depend on even Scripture to ease our fear of death.

Several years ago, I talked with a dying woman—a loving grandmother and strong Christian believer. Cancer had devoured her, and she was fading fast. We talked for hours about her relationship with Jesus. We read Bible verses together that spoke of heaven, her future home. She seemed unafraid, confident, and ready to die. Just before we parted, however, she asked some questions that surprised me.

"I am dying, Denise," she said. "How can I show courage when I die? How do I know all those things Jesus said about salvation, eternal life, and heaven, are true? What if they're not true? How can I know for sure that they're true, and not just hopeful fantasy?"

I stopped and reflected on Jesus' question to his disciples when they feared the violent storm. "Where is your faith?" he asked them. And, for the first time, I understood that facing death doesn't take courage. It takes faith. God's Word, God's promises, and Christ's example teach us to have faith. And faith erases fear every time.

Are you afraid of death? Does it stay constantly on your mind and terrify you? Does the fear of death keep you from fully living your life? Surely, if you spend your time fearing death, you cannot fully live.

If you are a woman in Christ, you can depend on Scripture to overcome your fear of death. Throughout the Bible, God makes concrete promises about death. You can take great comfort that, when you face death, Jesus will face it with you. God's everlasting love will embrace you, and see you through it. Death will not separate you from his presence, love, or care (Rom. 8:38-9).

3

The Fear of Physical Harm, Violence, Hate Crime, and Evil

"The energy of violence moves through our culture ... nobody is untouched. Violence is a part of ... our species. It is around us, and it is in us."

Gavin De Becker, *The Gift of Fear*

We live in a violent world. We all face the possibility of unprovoked physical harm through violence and crime. We must be cautious and careful, but we need not be afraid. Fear of what might happen can keep us from living life to the full.

We often cannot help but be apprehensive when we hear stories of evil and violence all around us – like the story of the rape and death of Catherine "Kitty" Genovese, almost forty years ago on a sunny day in New York City. In broad daylight, with thirty-eight people watching, Kitty's attacker stabbed her thirty times. Not one person ran to her defense. Three dozen bystanders watched the bloody brutality and did nothing.[1] The unstopped, uninterrupted violence shocked a nation. And we think that if rape and violent death could happen to Kitty Genovese, it can happen to us.

---

1   BreakPoint with Charles Colson, "His Brother's Keeper," July 12, 2002.

And that thought causes us to fear the unexpected violence from another person.

We might allow such fears to keep us trembling inside our home's locked doors. Some of us already live in fortress-like homes, complete with multiple padlocks, alarm systems, camera monitors, gated entrances, etc. The potential of unprovoked violence and physical harm keep many women living in fear and anxiety. Random crime seems an ever-present risk as we live and shop and drive during the ordinary hours of everyday life.

Routinely we hear of school shooting sprees in quiet Amish communities and public school systems, of rifle rampages in office complexes, of parking lot muggings. Violence comes unexpectedly and from surprising sources.

But we mustn't allow fear of crime to prevent us from living the abundant life Christ promises us, his believing daughters. We can face this threat without fear, because we have the knowledge of God's protection, and we are equipped with the God-given wisdom to practice safety precautions. We can also:

1. Understand that advertisers use fear of violence to sell us products. Just look at all the products that fear sells: protective window bars, security video cameras, unbreakable steel doors, double-bolted locks, home alarm systems, motion-detector floodlights, identity theft protection, and driveway electronic gates. While it's smart to use precautions, we don't have to turn our homes into bastions and strong imprisoning citadels.

2. Stop watching violence-filled programming that Hollywood puts on our television and theater

screens. They play to our fears—all those things that terrify us. Producers incorporate violence, hate crimes, human cruelty, and demonic evil into films and television programs. They can distort our thinking and keep us awake a night. We can refuse to watch them, and instead choose those programs that edify us, strengthen us, and give us hope.

3. Realize that most things we fear will never happen. I chuckle when I remember the hysteria surrounding the minute between midnight December 31, 1999 and 12:01 a.m., January 1, 2000. Fear of a mysterious computer glitch sent Americans scurrying to their basements with life supplies of food, batteries, and cash. Some even bought shotguns to protect their supplies from thieves. Others sold their homes and moved to the mountains for protection. But 1999 quietly ticked into 2000, and nothing happened.

"I have come that they may have life," Jesus claimed, "and have it to the full" (John 10:10). We can't let fear of what might happen keep us from living life "to the [promised] full."

4

THE FEAR OF LOSING LOVED ONES

What do we mean by fear? One dictionary defines fear as an unexpected attack, anxiety, or agitation caused by the presence of nearness of danger, evil, or pain .... But most of us don't need a dictionary to tell us what fear is; we know it in far more personal terms.

Chip Ingram, *I Am With You Always: Experiencing God in Times of Need*

Do you fear losing someone dear to you? As you already know, loss is a part of life. But you need not fear loss. When you experience the loss of a loved one, God gives you the needed strength to cope with the loss—just at the moment you need it. I know this to be true through my own personal experience. And I know of many other women who also claim its truth.

The fear of loss can strangle you emotionally, filling you with constant anxiety and sadness, and robbing you of hope and joy.

I often meet Christian women who desperately fear the loss (by death) of parents, friends, family members, and (if a wife and mother) a husband and children. The married woman might also worry about loss due to divorce or spouse abandonment.

A single young woman admitted to me that she dreaded her parents' routine doctor's visits each year. She feared physicians might find a tumor or disease that would handicap or kill them.

A forty-one-year-old wife told me recently: "I fear something is going to happen to my husband. The fear debilitates me. It keeps me from enjoying life. I fear he'll be killed in a car crash or job accident. I'm afraid to live without him. I just don't know what I would do."

One women I know fears daily for her marriage. "At the deepest level," she admits, "I fear rejection. I worry about being abandoned by my closest friend—my husband—as he is my most significant relationship."

The fear of divorce keeps some Christian women wrapped up in fear. Worry interrupts their daily lives, and often causes them to express themselves to their spouse in ways that damage the marriage. A frightened woman can emotionally overreact to innocent situations, or cling to a mate and never allow him out of her sight. She might hold onto him so tightly, she smothers him emotionally. She herself can bring his rejection—the very result she most fears.

Some women fear losing their children. They are afraid of all those dangers that can steal a child from them: death, injury, illness, kidnapping, drugs, violence, and school shootings. They "turn on their fear" the moment their children walk out the door for the day.

"I fear my son will be taken from me, either by kidnapping or by accident," one young mother told me.

Another admits: "My son is four, and he is so friendly and trusting, I'm afraid he'd be an easy target for a kidnapper."

Mothers continually hear of kidnappings and killings of children broadcast on the evening news. We yearn to protect our children from all those who might want to exploit and hurt them.

36

We also live in a culture where HIV, AIDS, and other diseases/pandemics compete for our children's health. We can keep our kids clean, vaccinated, and medically checked, but we are powerless to protect them from every germ and infection in society.

Though we have good reason to fear for the safety and good health of our children, we must remind ourselves that God's love and care are stronger than our fears, for as Christian believers, we know God is in control of life and death.

> "The God of Abraham, Isaac, and Jacob reigns...his plan and purposes rob the future of its fear."[1]

God also loves our children. He loves them more than you or I ever could. God is your child's ultimate Parent. You and I are but temporary caretakers.

When the worst happens, God stays close with his strength and comfort. He walks with us through the painful crisis. God makes us a promise: "Never will I leave you; never will I forsake you" (Heb. 13:5). When Jesus walks with us, we can weather any storm.

---

1   Charles Colson, statement from his *Templeton Address*, September 2, 1993.

5

FEAR – THE NUMBER ONE EMOTIONAL ISSUE FOR WOMEN

A major ministry organization's survey of more than fifteen thousand Christians showed that fear is the number one emotional issue for women. And that was before 9/11.

Cheri Fuller, *Fearless.*

Women today fear many things: The future. Disease and disfigurement. Mental illness. Loneliness and isolation. Failure, risk, rejection, ridicule, and embarrassment. They fear lack of productivity and accomplishment, or not measuring up to roles and responsibilities. They fear poverty and homelessness, aging and losing their independence. As odd as it may sound, some women even fear fear!

Throughout history, women have been stricken by disfigurement, death, and disease. Consider:

◊ In the fourteenth century, Black Death struck Europe, and wiped out one-third of its population.

◊ In the New World, during the time of Cortez, seventeen million Indians died from smallpox.

◊ In the early twentieth century, the flu epidemic killed thirty million people in Europe, Asia, Australia and the Americas.

◊ Today, AIDS is ravaging Africa. Disease control experts expect fifty-five million Africans to die from AIDS by 2020.[1]

Being alive means being at risk.

Recently I spoke with a Christian woman who feared growing old and losing her independence.

"I want to be able to think for myself and make my own decisions when I'm old," she said. "I don't want my children making decisions about my care, or deciding where I should live. I want the presence of mind to know when I need to move into an assisted living facility, and to have the financial means to live in a safe, clean, and caring environment."

While these might be concerns that you prepare for, they shouldn't be labeled "fears." Legitimate concerns lead to preventative action. They cause you to plan wisely, put money into savings accounts, and write a will. Fear, however, brings paralysis. It causes panic, angst, and anxiety. Fear muddles minds and emotions. It keeps you from making smart moves and wise decisions.

Different seasons of a woman's life can bring particular fears. For instance:

◊ Women in their 20s might fear college test grades, financial concerns, vocational choices, not finding the "right" husband or finding the "wrong" husband, and/or living a lifetime of singleness.

◊ The 30-something woman may have fears about marriage, vocation, infertility, planned and unplanned pregnancies, miscarriages, and caring for infants and young children.

---

1   "The African AIDS Crisis," BreakPoint WorldView, May 2003, p. 29.

◊ The middle-aged woman may fear for her children's education, safety, and life choices. She may be afraid for her (or her spouse's) health, the coming of menopause, her aging parents, limited retirement income, and future plans.

◊ The senior adult woman may fear loneliness, the empty nest, isolation from family and friends, disease and increased health concerns, aging and physical/mental limitations, financial and housing needs, death, and life after death. She may fear for her married sons and daughters, and her grandchildren.

◊ The elderly woman may shut down living and involving herself in activities. She may not start new ventures because she fears not being able to finish them. She may resist making new friends because she fears future emotional hurt from loss. Her fear of relational pain might be stronger than her fear of loneliness and isolation. "Many adults are cautious of attempting to build deep relationships with people because they fear making themselves vulnerable to emotional hurt," writes George Barna.[2]

◊ Other women are burdened by fears of personal inadequacies, and not measuring up to expected roles and responsibilities. They fear disappointing those loved ones who depend on them, or who look up to them with admiration; living life in discontentment; or feeling insignificant.

For women who put their value in fame, fortune, and status—and don't achieve them—discontentment can hit them hard in mid-life. Author Gustave Flaubert captured this deep discontent

---

2   George Barna, *If Things Are So Good, Why Do I Feel So Bad?* (Chicago: Moody Press, 1994), p. 128.

more than a hundred years ago, when he described his restless, unhappy, unfulfilled character, Madame Emma Bovary:

"Deep down ... she was waiting for something to happen. Like a sailor in distress, she kept casting desperate glances over the solitary waste of her life, seeking some white sail in the distant mists of the horizon. She had no idea by what wind it would reach her, toward what shore it would bear her, or what kind of craft it would be—tiny boat or towering vessel, laden with heartbreaks or filled to the gunwales with rapture."[3]

Madame Bovary's discontent results in a disastrous marriage, an adulterous affair, the mutilation of a young boy's leg, and her own tragic suicide.

You need not fear the future with its unknown mysteries because:

◊ God knows the future. Your Father knows the prospective happenings of every moment of time. His Word tells you to trust him with the past, present, and future.

◊ God gives you a purpose for the future. You'll have little time to worry when you concentrate on serving him, devoting yourself to prayer, and thanking him for his constant care (Col. 3:24; 4:2).

◊ God has been faithful in the past. He's kept you safe so far. And he promises to be with you as you journey through the rest of your life.

When women make service to God and others, prayer, and thanksgiving the first three emotional issues in their lives, fear and worry take a backseat.

---

3   Gustave Flaubert, *Madame Bovary* (Franklin Center, PA: The Franklin Library, 1979), p. 75.

SECTION 2

EXAMINE YOUR FEARS – HEALTHY FEAR, GOD'S GIFT THAT ARMS YOU

6

WISE WOMEN FEAR GOD

A woman who fears the Lord is to be praised.

Proverbs 31:30

What does this mean—wise women fear God? The fear of God is a healthy fear. It means you have a genuine respect for God, a deep reverence for His holiness. Scripture tells us to "fear" God. Does "fearing God" mean we should be afraid of him? Or scared that He'll send a lightning bolt our way if we step out of line? Didn't Jesus say: "Do not be afraid of those who kill the body but cannot kill the soul. Rather, be afraid of the One who can destroy both soul and body in hell" (Matt. 10:28)? Did Jesus mean we should quake and tremble when we approach the Lord in prayer – that we should fear his anger? I don't think so.

In this case, "fear" means reverence, respect, and obedience. As Christian believers, we're told to revere, respect, and obey God. He is our holy, all-powerful Creator. We are his creatures. We must hold God in awe and worship him. He holds our lives in his hands—our past, our present, and our future. He is the Vine that sustains us, the branches. Fearing God—who is a loving Father—is a healthy fear and respect. This healthy fear draws us toward God. It doesn't push us away from him. God has demonstrated his great love and concern for us by sending his Son, Jesus, to bridge the separating gap sin has caused between the Creator and us, his creatures (see John 3:16). Fearing God is healthy fear.

Solomon, one of Scripture's wisest characters, said: "Here is my final conclusion: Fear God and obey his commands, for this is the duty of every person" (Eccles. 12:13 NLT).

Fearing God is our duty and our delight. Our reverence for God takes away fears of violators, disease, divorce, discontent, isolation, lack of purpose, and everything else that threatens to scare and overwhelm us.

"The remarkable thing about fearing God," writes Oswald Chambers, "is that when you fear God you fear nothing else, whereas if you do not fear God you fear everything else."[1]

How true!

In ancient days, when the children of Israel wandered the desert on the way to the Promised Land, God instructed Moses to tell his people to "fear the Lord your God as long as you live by keeping all his decrees and commands...so that you may enjoy long life" (Deut. 6:2). He also commanded his creatures to love him: "Love the Lord your God with all your heart and with all your soul and with all your strength" (v. 5). Fear and love, according to Scripture, enfold each other like two lovers' hands.

Scripture tells us God blesses those who fear him. The psalmists write: "Blessed are all who fear the Lord, who

---

1   From Inspiration/Motivational Quotes and Sayings, November 8, 2003, online at http://openmind.org/SP/Quotes.htm

walk in his ways (Ps. 128:1), and "Happy are those who fear the Lord. Yes, happy are those who delight in doing what he commands" (112:1 NLT).

"People who fear God obey Him; they keep his commandments ... In other words, their obedience is not a grudging or forced obedience. They don't serve Him or walk in His ways because they have to, but because they want to. God-fearing people obey God because they consider it a privilege to please Him."[2]

Scripture also tells us that "godly wisdom" comes from fearing God. "The fear of the Lord is the beginning of wisdom; all who follow his precepts have good understanding," writes the psalmist (Ps. 111:10).

Wisdom is a quality that Scripture tells us to desire, to grow into, and to pray to receive. Consider the following Scriptural advice:

> Paul writes that in Christ "are hidden all the treasures of wisdom and knowledge." (Col. 2:3)

> Proverbs tells us that the "woman of noble character" possesses wisdom: "She speaks with wisdom, and faithful instruction is on her tongue." (Prov. 31:26)

> The writer of James compares believers who lack wisdom to "a wave of the sea, blown and tossed by the wind." (James 1:6) He urges Christians: "If you need wisdom—if you want to know what God wants you to do—ask him, and he will gladly tell you. He will not rebuke you for asking." (v. 5 NLT)

> Even Jesus—who was perfect—valued wisdom as he grew from child to adult: "So Jesus grew both in height

---

2   Wayne and Joshua Mack, The Fear Factor (Tulsa, OK: Hensley Publishing, 2002), p. 179.

and in wisdom, and he was loved by God and by all who knew him." (Luke 2:52 NLT)

God has instilled within us the ability to "fear" him—to love, honor, respect, revere, and obey him. That is the first, and primary, healthy fear we must possess.

God has also instilled within us a second type of healthy fear. I call this healthy fear A.R.M.S., and it stands for

Alert

Response that

Motivates

Survival.

A.R.M.S. has a totally different meaning from the fear of God. A.R.M.S. is the gift God gives to keep us (and our loved ones) safe from predators and danger. When faced with immediate and present danger, A.R.M.S. automatically and involuntarily—in physical, mental, and emotional ways—kicks in and equips us to protect ourselves. God's gift of A.R.M.S. healthy fear can instantly change the "mild-mannered reporter" to "Superwoman"! Let's examine in more detail this special gift of healthy fear.

7

HEALTHY FEAR DEMANDS YOUR UNDIVIDED ATTENTION

Healthy fear is a physical, emotional, and mental response to immediate and present danger. Healthy fear can save your life.

In the previous chapter, we saw that A.R.M.S. is healthy fear's automatic alert response that motivates survival. We depend on A.R.M.S. when we are faced with immediate and present danger. It prepares us to make the life-saving decision to either fight the predator or run from it. It's called the "fight or flight" response.[1] (I might add that the "freeze" response can also be life-saving.) When A.R.M.S. healthy fear takes control, chemical changes involuntarily happen within your body. These responses are God-planted survival mechanisms. They demand your undivided attention, make you physically stronger, mentally sharper, and emotionally ready to make life-saving choices. Let's look at how quickly healthy fear can capture our attention.

---

1   Harvard physiologist Walter B. Cannon first described this "fight" or "flight" phenomenon in 1932. Rhonda Britten, *Fearless Living* (New York: Dutton, 2001), pp. 19-20.

Consider the prophet Daniel when Gabriel, God's messenger angel, suddenly appeared to him. Daniel immediately reacted. He confesses: "As [Gabriel] came near the place where I was standing, I was terrified and fell prostrate" (Dan. 8:16-26; 9:20-27). Daniel showed healthy fear when confronted by this awesome ("wonderful" and "terrible") angel of God. Daniel's body, mind, and emotions shouted: "Daniel, pay attention! This guy looks dangerous! Other worldly! Prepare to defend yourself!" By falling facedown, Daniel chose the "flee" response.

Consider Zechariah, as he stood by the right side of the altar of incense, when Gabriel appeared to him as well. "When Zechariah saw him, he was startled and was gripped with fear" (Luke 1:11-20). Zechariah was so terrified, Gabriel had to tell him, "Do not be afraid," before he could deliver his message. We do not know if Zechariah fell to the floor or tried to run away. But we do know he didn't choose to fight the angel. Healthy fear caused him to be "gripped with fear," and he probably chose the "freeze" response.

When, on that starlit night, an angel appeared to the shepherds out in the field near Jesus' birthplace, they came to a startled halt. Luke writes that "the glory of the Lord shone around them" and the shepherds "were terrified" (Luke 2:9). Again the angel said to them: "Do not be afraid. I bring you good news" (v. 10). No doubt, some of the shepherds fled, and others might have frozen. But not one of them chose to fight. Their heightened mental ability instantly told them they couldn't battle an angel and win.

Healthy fear causes us to stop, look, and listen. Daniel, Zechariah, and the shepherds had a good reason to give the messenger angels their focused attention. Listen to Daniel as he describes the physical appearance of the arch-angel, Michael (see Dan. 10:13).

"His body was like chrysolite," he says, "his face like lightning, his eyes like flaming torches, his arms and legs like the gleam of burnished bronze, and his voice like the sound of a multitude" (v. 6).

No wonder Daniel's face turned deathly pale, and his whole body trembled (vv. 8, 10). What did the angel tell him? "Do not be afraid, Daniel" (v. 12). And a second time the angel told him: "Do not be afraid, O man highly esteemed...Peace! Be strong now; be strong" (v. 19).

Zechariah was startled and gripped by fear when he saw the angel. Daniel turned deathly pale and his whole body trembled. The shepherds were terrified. At first appearance, they had no idea whether this mysterious being was friend or foe. At first sight of the angel, involuntary chemical changes happened in each body— changes that automatically prepared them to fight, flee, or freeze. Each person displayed the typical and healthy Alert Response (that) Motivates Survival-type fear. And each time, after a bout of healthy fear captured the person's full attention, the angel assured them he posed no danger, but had a message from God. Only then did they listen to what the angel had to say. In these cases, the fear that seemed so real, and so life-threatening, proved to be only imagined fear. But each body, mind, and emotion reacted to the fear with the same A.R.M.S. response.

What amazing changes happen within your body when you are confronted by a fearful sight or a life-threatening predator?

8

How Your Body Responds to Healthy Fear

[Speaking of the A.R.M.S. response] It is the most primal of survival mechanisms, not only in humans but in virtually all species ever studied for the fear response.

Rhonda Britten, *Fearless Living*

When my husband, Timothy, and I lived and worked in Chelsea, Massachusetts, a small and violent inner city on the outskirts of Boston, we learned a lot about the A.R.M.S. fear survival response. Gang violence, street stabbings, robbery, home invasions—we experienced all of them. A.R.M.S. probably kept us alive during those years of inner city ministry.[1] We learned to depend on our God-endowed fear instincts.

It's the shock factor of both healthy and unhealthy fear that stops us in our tracks and grabs our attention. Our immediate reaction is initially the same for both: undivided concentration of mind, body, and emotions. The difference between healthy and unhealthy fear is the purpose of the fear and our response to it. For instance:

---

1   I write about these frightening experiences in my book: *Johnny Cornflakes: A Story About Loving the Unloved*, Christian Focus Publishers, 2010.

◊ Healthy fear helps us to survive by causing us to react in safety-wise ways. For example: you hear a loud, frightening tornado siren and so decide to take protective cover. Or, the newspaper reports robberies in your neighborhood and so you lock your doors and take other safety precautions. Healthy fear on the streets of inner city Chelsea caused us to be aware at all times of everything happening around us. We did what we had to do in our ministry, but we knew that physical safety demanded constant alertness to our surroundings.

◊ Healthy fear protects us. But unhealthy fear can render us immobile, damage our minds and bodies (worry, anxiety, and other traits of unhealthy fear are harmful), and doesn't necessarily lead to our survival. For example, you hear of a kidnapping in another state, and become so anxious about your own child's safety that you worry constantly, and barely let her out of your sight. Or, an angry colleague casually, but jokingly, threatens you, and you become so fearful that you lie awake at night and won't go back to work. You just can't live a healthy, productive life if you allow unhealthy fears to pilot your daily life.

The Scriptures often record instances of men and women who experienced deep fright—from either healthy or unhealthy fear—and reacted with physical, chemical changes that involuntarily moved them into the healthy fear survival mode. For instance:

When Jesus was confronted by a detachment of weapon-carrying soldiers, chief priests, and Pharisees, he asked the men: "Who is it you want?" (John 18:4).

"Jesus of Nazareth," they replied. Jesus, having just risen from prayer, and not armed with any weapon, quietly announced to them: "I am he."

Suddenly, when these men who wanted to arrest Jesus realized they were looking directly at him, they became horribly frightened. Their bodies and minds responded to the chemical changes taking place within them. Expecting immediate danger, they actually "drew back and fell to the ground" (v. 6). In other words, they "fled."

And that's when Simon Peter's healthy fear alarm went off. He quickly drew his sword, struck the high priest's servant, cutting off his right ear (v. 10). Peter's "fight or flight" response told him to "fight."

I've often thought about Peter when Roman soldiers dropped him down into the deep hole of the sixth century B.C. Mamertine prison in Rome, at the foot of the Capitoline Hill. Many of Rome's prisoners starved and died deep inside the dark, damp underground cell, filled with rotting human corpses and flesh-eating rats. Stairs have since been built so that pilgrims can see where Peter spent his last days. I felt a certain "unsettledness" on the occasions I climbed down into the cell and reflected upon Peter, and the fear he must have felt there. History tells us that Peter spent some time in the twelve-foot deep prison before he was executed in Nero's circus on Vatican Hill.[2]

Scripture tells us that at the resurrection, on the first day of the week, very early in the morning, Mary Magdalene, Joanna, Mary the mother of James, and other women brought traditional burial spices to place on Jesus' body. When they arrived at Jesus' tomb, they found the

---

2   From personal experience, and found at: http://www.sacred-destinations.com/ italy/rome-mamertine-prison. Accessed: January 10, 2010.

huge stone door rolled away. They walked into the cave-like sepulcher, and saw two men "in clothes that gleamed like lightning" standing beside them (Luke 24:4). Within their bodies and minds, the women's healthy fear response screamed: "Danger! Prepare to fight, flee, or freeze!"

Luke tells us: "In their fright the women bowed down with their faces to the ground" (v. 5). In other words, they "fled." A.R.M.S. healthy fear, and the chemical changes in their bodies caused them to seek protection from perceived danger by falling down and covering their faces.

We can only imagine the fear felt by the centurions, soldiers, religious officials, and others who witnessed Jesus' death. Matthew describes the chaotic scene: "At that moment...the earth shook and the rocks split. The tombs broke open and the bodies of many holy people who had died were raised to life. They came out of the tombs" (Matt. 27:51-3). And the executioners' response? "They were terrified" (v. 54). They probably both "froze" and "fled"! The unbelieving blood-thirsty crowd even exclaimed: "Surely he was the Son of God!" (v. 54).

What happens inside your body when you face danger? All of a sudden, your heart races and beats wildly against your chest. Your blood pressure soars and substantially increases blood flow to your brain. You need the extra blood in "central control" because you are making a quick, life-saving decision: "Should I fight or should I flee?' The extra blood to your brain improves your decision-making faculties. At the same time, your blood sugar rises to supply more fuel for physical energy. Blood from your gut goes to the large muscles of your arms and legs. You might need the increased speed and strength the extra blood provides. Your blood is programmed to clot quicker, just in case your attacker tears your skin or causes you to hemorrhage. Within seconds, your instant wisdom, alertness, swiftness, and daring strength might surprise you.

No doubt, the passengers on Northwest Airlines Flight 253 used the healthy fear survival A.R.M.S. to jump Umar Farouk Abdulmutallab and stop him from blowing up their plane as they prepared to land in Detroit.

God equipped most all living creatures to respond to danger with the same healthy A.R.M.S. reaction. I can remember a time when our big, black outdoor cat, Shannon, Jr., came in contact with our neighbor's Doberman Pinscher. I saw the same survival response take over. Shannon Jr.'s back arched and pointed to the sky. Every hair on his body stood at attention. His eyes widened and his claws extended like switchblades. He looked like a Halloween cat in a child's coloring book. His entire body froze as he anticipated his next move—cat-fight, freeze, or tuck-his-tail-and-run flight.

The cat's body automatically armed (A.R.M.S.) itself to keep the Doberman from eating him. Since the cat was part "chicken"—and somewhat smart—he fled to the nearest tree, scurried to the top branch, and waited for the demonized dog to depart.

9

How A.R.M.S. Fear Can Save Your Life

For you created my inmost being, you knit me together in my mother's womb. I praise you because I am fearfully and wonderfully made.

Psalm 139:13-14

Have you ever faced such a terrifying predator that you discovered instant hidden strengths you never knew you possessed? Healthy fear's A.R.M.S. brings to the surface the strengths that lie dormant within you until you are confronted with catastrophe and desperately need these strengths.

Patricia Van Tighem discovered her hidden physical strengths, and increased mind alertness, when she and her newly wed husband, Trevor, took a hike in the Canadian Rockies. They were enjoying their walk together when a female grizzly bear ran toward him. The bear savagely attacked her unsuspecting husband, mauling him and tearing away part of his leg.

Patricia didn't know if her husband was dead or alive. The bear then charged toward Patricia. The young woman felt sheer terror. She describes her fear in her book, *The Bear's Embrace.*

"Seconds pass," she writes. "Time holds still. A grizzly? I take two steps back. Where am I going? What should I do? My heart beats loud in the silent, snowy woods."

Automatically Patricia's mind and body moved into A.R.M.S. mode. God's gift of healthy fear produced all the needed chemical changes that gave her mental alertness, extra strength, and more fuel to fight or flee. Wisely, she chose to flee. She ran as hard as she could and climbed up a tree. She waited in the thin top branches, unaware that grizzly bears can also climb trees. The bear followed her. It grabbed her, threw her to the ground, wrapped its massive jaws around her head, and began to gnaw her head "like a dog chews a bone."

The bear left Patricia for dead. She lay on the ground, bleeding, broken, but still barely breathing. Somehow both Patricia and Trevor survived the bear's attack. They spent the next decade, however, undergoing multiple surgeries, physical therapy, severe pain, and facial disfigurement.[1]

While Patricia suffered significant injuries, no doubt her quick healthy fear reaction saved her life. A human surviving a bear attack is a rare occurrence.

I saw this same quick response when my neighbor took her dog and young granddaughter for a walk. A truck came speeding down the road toward her granddaughter's stroller. My neighbor saw the truck, and, just in time, she pushed the stroller onto a lawn and jumped out of the truck's way. The dog wasn't so fortunate. The truck hit and killed him. But my neighbor's immediate healthy fear reaction saved two lives.

God equips his creatures to respond to immediate danger with the gift of healthy fear. Healthy fear seeks

---

1   Patricia Van Tighem, *The Bear's Embrace* (New York: Pantheon Books, 2001), pp. 16-18.

to remove/destroy the danger (fight), or to remove you from the danger (flight). By giving you the gift of healthy fear, God equips you for survival. Remember that healthy fear arms you. It is your God-given healthy Alert Response (that) Motivates Survival. A.R.M.S. makes you immediately multitalented and able to multitask. Your mind and muscles spring instantly to life when you face dangerous circumstances. You can depend on your innate God-endowed survival response to help preserve your life and the lives of those you love.

This is good news! A.R.M.S. can keep you from fearing danger. For when, and if, danger threatens you, God-given healthy fear will equip you to deal with it. You can count on it.

When I read about the heroic abilities of a soldier in Iraq when Jihad mercenaries ambushed his division, I recognized both healthy fear's rapid response, and how combat training equips a soldier to react immediately. His tank on fire, Lance Corporal Billy W. Peixotto took charge of his terrifying situation with the help of A.R.M.S. healthy fear. It gave him super strength, quick decision-making ability, and the speed to perform many dangerous things at once.

Peixotto climbed out of his burning vehicle while enemies fired at him with automatic weapons and rocket-propelled grenades. He grabbed the tank's exterior fire extinguishers and put out the blaze that threatened the lives of his crew members. With the help of Captain Jeffrey Houston, he removed the tank's leaking exterior fuel bladder to prevent additional fires. Then Peixotto "zigzagged like a broken-field runner" back to his tank and unsuccessfully tried to restart and move it. When Peixotto saw that Houston had been seriously wounded, he jumped from the tank and rushed to his side. While the enemy still fired slugs and rockets, the young marine pulled his fallen company commander to safety by the side of the tank, and administered life-saving first aid.

While he applied pressure to Houston's head wound (to keep him from going into shock or bleeding to death), Peixotto fired at the enemy with his M9 9mm pistol. When Captain Dave Bardorf led doctors to the rescue, he described Peixotto's superhuman feats:

"It was incredible," Bardorf said. "He [Peixotto] was slowing the blood flow with one hand, laying fire on the enemy with the others, and directing fire from a radio another Marine held for him."

Healthy fear came to Peixotto's rescue, and helped save his life and the lives of his crew.

For his "heroic achievement," the Marine Corps awarded Peixotto the Bronze Star for Valor.[2]

Both Patricia Van Tighem and Billy Peixotto were enabled to more fully protect themselves and others thanks to healthy fear's involuntary survival responses. While one fled and one fought, each discovered a supernatural strength in muscle, uncommon intelligence of mind, and roadrunner swiftness to action. It's the same response that make a mother instinctively dial 911 when she finds her baby not breathing, or sees her husband grab his heart in pain, or hears her elderly mother fall down the stairs. A.R.M.S. works in bear attacks, enemy attacks, and also in everyday crises. A.R.M.S. is the healthy fear that promises to protect us and others. We can thank God for this healthy fear survival tool.

---

2   David H. Hackworth, "The Few, the Proud, and the Under-Rewarded," quoted from WorldNetDaily online, October 7, 2003.

10

You Are Created To Survive

The angel of the Lord encamps around those who fear him, and he delivers them.

Psalm 34:7

Healthy fear always takes action when danger arises. But after the danger disappears, and your safety has been achieved, you move quickly out of the A.R.M.S. mode and return to normal. Your body may be exhausted, but feelings of anxiety don't linger. The work of healthy fear is done. It has protected you and maybe even saved your life.

But what happens when the fear and anxiety remain after the threat has passed? Physiologically speaking, your body stays in the A.R.M.S. fear mode. Your heart still races. Your blood pressure still soars. Extra blood continues to flow to your brain and rush to the large muscles of your arms and legs. Your blood sugar steadily rises, filling your body with more fuel for physical energy. Your brain continues to shout again and again to your body: "C'mon! Hurry up! Make your decision! Fight or flee! I'm ready! I'm waiting! What will it be?"

How long do you think you could endure this heightened alert level? What would happen to your body, mind, and emotions if you remained in the A.R.M.S. fear mode for a long time, maybe for the rest of your life? Would you die? Would you go into shock? Would your body wear out like your car would if you accelerated to ninety miles per hour standing still with your brake on? The obvious answer is that you cannot endure such long-term stress without becoming ill. In this case, when the symptoms of healthy fear don't leave, God's gift of healthy fear has been displaced by Satan's imposter, an unhealthy fear potentially more dangerous than the original threat.

Unlike healthy fear, which is your God-given gift that arms you with extraordinary strength to fight or flee from the predator who stands ready to attack you, unhealthy fear is that unfounded fear that keeps your body in alert response, and continues to motivate survival long after the threat has subsided.

Let me illustrate with the story of David, the shepherd boy. David possessed a good sense of healthy fear when he stood before the mighty Goliath. The nine-foot-tall Philistine challenged Israel:

"Choose a man and have him come down to me. If he is able to fight and kill me, we will become your subjects; but if I overcome him and kill him, you will become our subjects and serve us" (1 Sam. 17:8).

Scripture says that on hearing the Philistine's words, "Saul and all the Israelites were dismayed and terrified" (v. 11). This is healthy fear. They had good reason to be "dismayed and terrified" of Goliath—especially when they did not consider God in the equation. They fled. Jesse's son, David, from Bethlehem, however, took the challenge. (This is faith in the face of healthy fear. He chose to fight.)

"Who is this uncircumcised Philistine that he should defy the armies of the living God?" the boy asked (v. 26). And to King Saul, he announced, "The Lord who delivered me from the paw of the lion and the paw of the bear will deliver me from the hand of this Philistine" (v. 37).

Without armor and holding a single slingshot, David decided to fight the Philistine—who had armored himself from head to toe with 125 pounds of bronze and carried a 15-pound iron-tipped spear.

"You have come against me with sword and spear and javelin," David said to the Philistine, "but I come against you in the name of the Lord Almighty, the God of the armies of Israel, whom you have defied" (v. 45).

As a laughing Goliath moved closer to attack him, God's gift of healthy fear armed David to think clearly, and to aim his sling accurately at the giant's brow. Healthy fear gave the boy the necessary strength to plant the stone firmly into the giant's forehead. David killed Goliath, and with the Philistine's own sword, he cut off his head (vv. 49-51).

Healthy fear A.R.M.S. you to meet a dangerous challenge, like Goliath, with extra strength, keener thinking, and superhuman swiftness. When the giant falls down dead, when you are once again safe, your body changes back to normal.

Unhealthy fear, however, physically and mentally prepares you, day after day, to kill a headless giant who no longer threatens you. Unhealthy fear harms you.

A major purpose of this book is to teach you to distinguish between God's gift of healthy fear and Satan's tool of unhealthy fear.

SECTION 3

UNHEALTHY FEAR –
SATAN'S TOOL THAT HARMS YOU

11

Unhealthy Fear is Satan's Instrument

We know that we are children of God, and that the whole world is under the control of the evil one. We know also that the Son of God has come and has given us understanding, so that we may know him who is true.

1 John 5:19-20

Unhealthy fear is a physical, emotional, and mental response to a "shadow" fear. A shadow fear represents no immediate or present danger because it originates in our mind. By habit and/or past conditioning, our body moves into A.R.M.S., but for no actual life-saving cause. If A.R.M.S. stands for:

Alert
Response (that)
Motivates
Survival.

Then I will call this unhealthy fear response: H.A.R.M.S:

Harmful
Alert
Response (that)
Mimics
Survival (reaction).

One (A.R.M.S.) response "motivates" survival and can save your life. The other (H.A.R.M.S.) "mimics" the A.R.M.S. survival reaction and can damage you.

Anxiety produced by unhealthy fear "harms" us. Manufactured by Satan, it mocks God's beautiful gift of survival—the A.R.M.S. fear reaction. H.A.R.M.S. pretends to help, but it's a phony. It's useless. It most often comes to us in mild bouts of panic and anxiety, sleeplessness, or perpetual unpleasant thoughts of what "might" happen. In serious unhealthy situations, we can experience more extreme reactions of fear, including panic attack, post-traumatic stress disorder, full-blown anxiety, and phobia.

H.A.R.M.S. will sidetrack your own personal ministry, will self-destruct your body, confuse your mind, shatter your emotions, dilute your belief in God's Word, question God's promises, and keep you from actively working for God's kingdom purposes. You'll spend your prime time running away from a bear that's not even there. If not relieved over a period of time, unhealthy fear's reaction will certainly harm you. It might even destroy you.

Satan's attack on your life through unhealthy fear reactions can be compared to Dutch elm disease's attack on the American elm tree. During the past seventy years, the disease has killed more than seventy million elm trees (ninety-five per cent of all elms) in the United States alone. The Dutch elm disease fungus is a silent killer that attacks the elm and clogs its water-conducting vessels. The elm's strong roots continue to send water to the trunk, but the clogged vessels keep the branches from receiving the water. The mightiest elm can die in as little as three weeks. The disease spreads quickly, and taints tree after tree until an entire neighborhood or forest of elms dies. For without needed water from its roots, the elm tree cannot survive.

Similarly, unhealthy fear severs your dependence on God's Word. It clogs your belief that God is in control. It makes you question whether or not God is able to protect and care for you, as well as for your loved ones. It interrupts the creature-Creator free flow of prayer and intimacy. You are still his daughter, of course, but Satan's tool of unhealthy fear distracts you from feeling secure in Christ.

You can see Satan's first attack with unhealthy fear in Genesis 3:10. God had created a beautiful, safe world for Adam and Eve. He had placed them in a perfect garden to live and love and walk daily with him.

"The Lord God made all kinds of trees grow out of the ground—trees that were pleasing to the eye and good for food" (Gen. 2:9).

In the middle of the garden, however, God planted the "tree of the knowledge of good and evil," and he told Adam not to eat its fruit (v. 17).

That's when Satan, in the form of a snake, planted a moment of unhealthy doubt and fear within Eve's mind. He caused her to question her Creator when he announced: "God knows that when you eat of it your eyes will be opened, and you will be like God, knowing good and evil" (Gen. 3:5).

Eve gave in to her anxiety. She feared "not knowing," and living the rest of her life with her eyes closed. She took a bite of the forbidden fruit. Then she convinced Adam to eat it too (v. 6).

When God came to them for their afternoon walk, the frightened couple hid. God called to Adam: "Where are you?" (v. 9)

Adam answered him, and for the first time in the Bible, we hear the word "afraid."

"I heard you in the garden," Adam told the Lord, "and I was afraid...so I hid" (v. 10).

Adam blamed his eating on Eve. Eve blamed her appetite on the serpent. But, at that moment, the disease called "sin" severed the branches from its Root. The couple in paradise died spiritually. And unhealthy fear was born.

The "sin" disease spread quickly, and tainted being after being until the entire race of people died spiritually. For sin clogged the vessels that carried spiritual water from the Root to its branches, and without spiritual water, the beings couldn't survive.

Unhealthy fear—Satan's tool—has plagued humanity from the first human being.

That's the bad news. Since Adam and Eve, we all have "clogged vessels." But God gives us good news too. It's the same news Jesus gave to a Samaritan woman at Jacob's well. This woman lived life weighed down by multiple loads of unhealthy fear. Hurt by life, and a battery of abusive husbands, she feared yet another abandonment, another hardship of insecurity, loneliness, and isolation. She came to the well at noon, the hottest hour. She came alone. She had no friends. She dodged the town's women who came to draw water in the cool of the morning or evening. They hated her and gossiped behind her back.

What did Jesus give her? Water. Living water. He forever removed the clog that stopped her from receiving life-sustaining water from God. He offered her Living Water that would forever flow freely through her heart.

"Whoever drinks the water...will never thirst," Jesus told her. "Indeed, the water I give...will become...a spring of water welling up to eternal life" (John 4:14).

So sick with the disease of sin, she gulped down his Living Water. And the Samaritan woman—the dead branches with the wilted leaves—sprang to life. So filled with Living Water, she ran back to town, shared the Water, and immediately produced fruit—in the form of converts—for Christ.

"Many of the Samaritans from that town believed in him [Jesus] because of the woman's testimony," John writes (v. 39).

Unhealthy fear no longer weighed down upon her. She had found freedom through Christ.

As a believer in Christ, you too have flowing within you that life-sustaining Living Water. You need not suffer from unhealthy fear. You are firmly attached to the Root, and Christ's Living Water flows through you unhindered.

How can we tell the difference between healthy fear—God's gift that arms you—and unhealthy fear—Satan's tool that harms you? First, let's look at the results of unhealthy fear on our bodies, minds, and souls.

12

WOMEN AND PANIC ATTACKS

The emotional response of fear is always preceded by a thought, although it can be so rapid that you're hardly aware of the connection.

Neil T. Anderson and Rich Miller, *Freedom from Fear*

Perhaps you are old enough to remember the summer of 1962 when the Soviet Union moved nuclear missiles into Cuba. These missiles, armed and aimed, had the capacity to strike the United States with little warning. The Cuban Missile Crisis upset President John F. Kennedy, other United States leaders, and every average American citizen.

I remember that Crisis. I was eleven years old and in the sixth grade. It lasted almost two weeks before finally resolved without bloodshed. So afraid of a nuclear attack from Cuba, our elementary school teachers taught us to duck down under our school desks, cover our heads with our hands, and stay still until the drill ended. We practiced many times throughout school days. The alarm sounded, and we ducked and covered our heads.

This sounds so silly today when I tell my own children about the drills. Why we ever thought the "duck and cover" method might save our lives from a nuclear attack, I don't know. But, long after the Crisis passed, and we were once again "at relative peace" with Cuba and the Soviet Union, I continued to fear a nuclear attack. A loud noise, sounding like a drill alarm, would send me ducking under a piece of furniture, and sent my hands instinctively to my head. For a long time, I feared Cuba's missiles, even though they had been dismantled and the conflict solved.

The healthy fear reaction prompted when I heard the drill's alarm, became the unhealthy fear response after the threat had ended.

Oftentimes, panic attacks or panic disorders result from unhealthy fear responses. A panic attack or disorder is a "disabling mental condition that causes frightening... physical symptoms such as pounding heart, shortness of breath, and the feeling of losing control or dying."[1]

Panic refers to fear that is sudden, extreme, and completely groundless. The word comes from "Pan"—a Greek mythological "god" of the forests and meadows. Shepherds in ancient Greece worshiped Pan—portrayed as half man and half goat—because they believed he protected their flocks and herds. Pan—depicted with goat feet, curly hair, short horns, and beard—caused great, sudden, and groundless fear by his sudden and strange appearance.

I experienced my first real panic attack the summer of 1976 in New York City. I took visiting friends sightseeing that weekend and they wanted to see the Statue of Liberty. When we arrived, my friends insisted we climb up to her crown. During those days, climbing up to her torch was no longer allowed. I didn't want to admit it to them, but

---

1   "Panic Disorder," WebMD with AOL Health, October 21, 2003.

I was terrified of heights. Climbing atop a chair to change a ceiling light bulb was about as high as I ever wanted to go. And even doing that made my heart beat faster.

I finally agreed to climb up a few stairs with them inside Lady Liberty. I assured myself I could turn around and return to solid ground at any stage in the journey. Little did I know that the stairs were one-way—straight up. Turning around on the people-packed, narrow ladder was not possible. Not quite one-third of the way up, inside the statue's flowing skirts, I suddenly froze. I couldn't move—not up or down. I white-knuckled the railing. I broke out in a hot sweat all over my body. I felt nauseated. My heart raced, and my entire body trembled. I have never been so frightened, so paralyzed, in my life. I can't even begin to describe the fear I felt deep within the loins of Lady Liberty. My entire body reacted as if I had suddenly faced Goliath himself. I clamped shut my eyes. One friend had to pull me, and the other friend push me until I somehow slowly crawled up to her crown and back down to the ground.

I never again attempted to climb the Statue of Liberty. This past Christmas, however, my son, Christian, and his wife, Rebecca, and I climbed up the narrow, steep rock-hewn steps to the lookout post of the old fortress atop a mountain in Assisi, Italy. I took one stair at a time with Christian behind me and Rebecca in front of me. Slowly I ascended to the roof. I was in no danger of falling because there was no place to fall. Christian and Rebecca supported me, front and back. But I still experienced the racing heart, shortness of breath, and sweaty hands. And I felt relieved to put my feet back on Assisi's solid ground. The experience proved yet another episode I experienced with unhealthy fear. I couldn't have reacted any worse than if I had teetered atop a narrow ledge with no support. The physical reaction was the same.

Unhealthy fear can cause panic attacks. In the crown of Lady Liberty, I was safely protected by steel railings. But my body reacted as if I stood at the edge of a mountain precipice with one foot on ice and the other foot on air.

Let me give you another example of panic attack. Imagine you are walking a trail in Indonesia—the home of the largest known snake. Without warning, you stumble onto the forty-nine-foot-long python—all 990 pounds of him. You know he is capable of swallowing a full-grown sheep, and has also eaten his fair share of humans.[2] What would you do?

Healthy fear would race your heart, raise your blood pressure, send needed blood to your brain and large muscles, and shout the question and advice: "fight or flight?! Call it quick!" It would prepare your body for survival—A.R.M.S. Healthy fear would advise you to run away before you became the snake's snack.

A panic attack brings on the same physical changes as healthy fear, and shouts the same life-saving question— "fight or flight?"—but no snake exists. You face no real danger—just imagined danger. But the physical response is the same.

Fear that does not result in saving your life against a real threat is not healthy fear. Healthy fear responds only to real danger. Unhealthy fear, in the form of a panic attack, responds physically to the thought of physical threat. Do you see the difference?

No one completely understands what causes panic

2   "Indonesia Claims to Have Largest Snake," Associated Press, from chicagotribune. com, December 30, 2003.

disorders. Some believe they are caused by an imbalance of brain chemicals, or passed down through families, or triggered by stressful events. Panic attacks can cause you to have feelings of intense terror, choking, and "going crazy." They can produce chest pain or tightness, breathing difficulty, dizziness, sweating, shaking, chills or hot flashes, lightheadedness, and nausea.

Even the threat of a sudden panic attack can cripple some women as they perform their daily activities. Panic disorder is twice as common in women as men.[3]

In her book *Triumph Over Fear*, author Jerilyn Ross describes her first panic attack. While she vacationed in Salzburg, Austria, she felt a sudden rush of terror.

"I felt I was in terrible danger," she writes. "Suddenly I felt as if a magnet was pulling me toward the edge of the room.... Everything started to spin. I felt as though I was on the verge of completely losing control of myself...like being in a vacuum or in the middle of a tornado."[4]

Jerilyn describes how she broke out in a cold sweat and her heart pounded. She experienced more panic attacks throughout the following days and months. She later discovered that the fear of heights (acrophobia) caused her panic disorder. When she rode an elevator above the tenth floor in an office building or restaurant, her thought-system's automatic "red alert" told her body to fight or flee—a false A.R.M.S. alarm. Remember, H.A.R.M.S. mimics A.R.M.S.

Perhaps you, like Jerilyn, have experienced a panic

---

3   "Panic Disorder," WebMD with AOL Health, October 21, 2003.

4   Jerilyn Ross, *Triumph Over Fear* (New York: Bantam Books, 1994), p. 5.

attack. No doubt, it frightened you, and you thought your life was at risk. But experts tell us that while the fear during an attack is real, raw, crushing, and overwhelming, and the urge to escape is irresistible and not imaginary, panic attacks are not life-threatening.[5]

When panic attacks you, and you feel the fear of losing physical and emotional control, you can find help. You need not allow panic disorder to interfere with your life, work, relationships, and personal ministry. You can overcome this unhealthy fear. You can find relief from it. Through counseling, Jerilyn found relief and recovered. Find a good Christian counselor, one that comes highly recommended by your pastor, friend, or family member, and allow her to help you face and fight this unhealthy fear.

Some Christian women think that to seek counseling means they lack faith in God to heal them. This is untrue. Sometimes we all need the assistance of a trained Christian counselor to ask us the right questions, to guide us through a scriptural understanding of our problems, and to show us how to work through our fears. There is nothing "un-Christian" about seeking help.

---

5   Jerilyn Ross, *Triumph Over Fear*, Ibid., p. 19.

13

WOMEN AND POST-TRAUMATIC STRESS DISORDER

Post-traumatic stress disorder is an anxiety disorder that's triggered by your memories of a traumatic event—an event that directly affected you or an event that you witnessed.

MayoClinic.com

Have you ever experienced an accident, beating, rape, or other traumatic episode that stayed on your mind for months, maybe years, after the experience? If so, you might be suffering from post-traumatic stress disorder, another unhealthy fear that can wreck your daily life and hinder your work.

If you are the survivor of a traumatic event, such as a concentration camp, war horror, torture, school shooting, earthquake, hurricane or tornado, sexual assault, car or plane crash, or hostage situation, you may experience vivid and distressing memories of the event. In fact, it would be unusual if you didn't.

In the book *The Secret Holocaust Diaries*, my friend and co-author, Carolyn Tomlin, and I wrote the story of Nonna Bannister, a woman from the Ukraine who survived Hitler's concentration camps. After the war, Nonna came to the United States, and met her future husband, Henry Bannister. They married, had children, and lived a predictable and normal life. But, so horrific were Nonna's memories of World War II, of German soldiers killing her father, of work camps, of losing her mother and other family members, she couldn't bring herself to talk about it. Only a few years before her death, in 2004, was Nonna finally able to tell Henry—her husband of almost fifty years – about her past pain.

You see, when your mind recalls the traumatic experience you suffered, you not only remember it, but you relive it as well. Symptoms typically coming within several months after the event may include nightmares or flashbacks, trouble sleeping, problems with anger, and difficulty concentrating. You may be hypersensitive to noise and experience increased blood pressure, rapid heart rate, rapid breathing, nausea, and diarrhea. You may feel hopeless about the future.[1] Know that "fear is one of the most difficult emotions with which victims must come to terms. Reliving the experience sometime after the crime, the victim may be able to feel the intensity of the terror for the first time."[2]

Patricia Van Tighem, whose mauling by a grizzly bear almost killed her, suffered severe post-traumatic stress disorder. She writes:

"I am so afraid in the world. Afraid that the house will be broken into, afraid to walk in the park with my children, afraid to drive on busy roads. It feels constantly as if something else is going to happen to me.... I have

---

1   "Post-Traumatic Stress Disorder," MayoClinic.com, October 22, 2003, online.

2   Morton Bard and Dawn Sangrey, *The Crime Victim's Book* (New York: Basic Books, Inc., 1979), p. 42.

nightmares of being attacked...they plague me, awake and asleep."[3]

For twenty years after the bear attack, Patricia tried to "curb these horrible dark feelings and fears." She admitted: "I just want to shut off. But I can't."

To rid herself of haunting memories and fears, Patricia tried antidepressants and saw a counselor. She tried stress therapy, sound and light therapy, the yeast diet, acupuncture, craniosacral therapy, reflexology, and megavitamins. She recorded her dreams, regressed to childhood, and listened to relaxation tapes. She spent long days in a psychiatric hospital. Patricia spent years in her search for healing. She admits that she finally found some healing by breaking down her days into manageable pieces, and spending more time with her husband and children.

If you are a victim of haunting fears that traumatize you with life-interfering memories, I urge you to get help. While loved ones can help you heal in many areas of your life, professional and medical help from physicians, mental health workers, and/or trained Christian counselors will ensure your healing. You can also know that God, who knows your thoughts and experiences (see Ps. 139), can transform your mind, renew your spirit, and guide you into a future free from unhealthy fear. Don't allow post-traumatic stress disorder to disrupt your daily life, work, and relationships. You can receive help and hope.

---

3   Patricia Van Tighem, *The Bear's Embrace* (New York: Pantheon Books, 2001), p. 194.

14

WOMEN AND ANXIETY

Fear is an emotional reaction to a specific real or unreal danger, such as vicious dogs or goblins, whereas anxiety denotes a general gloomy feeling of impending doom.

Dr Benjamin B. Wolman, *Children's Fears*

We've talked about how healthy fear "is a momentary reaction to danger...based on a low estimate of one's own power as compared to the power of the threatening factor," and how it disappears when the threat disappears. Anxiety is different from healthy fear. Anxiety, an unhealthy fear, "is general and lasting. It has a feeling of no specific object but reflects overall weakness, ineptitude, and helplessness. Anxiety...can paralyze one's life."[1]

If you suffer from anxiety, you will feel the uncomfortable feeling of fear that never seems to go away. This type of fear can cause you to anticipate with dread that something awful is going to happen. It can have physical and emotional symptoms, some so severe they disrupt your daily life.

---

1   Dr Benjamin B. Wolman, *Children's Fears* (New York: Grosset & Dunlap, 1978), p. 18.

"A word we often interchange with fear is anxiety, which comes from the Latin *anxius*. To be anxious means 'to press tightly or to strangle.' Anxiety is often a suffocating experience."[2]

Laura Neuman, thirty-eight, never suffered the symptoms of post-traumatic stress disorder. But she did spend two decades living with severe anxiety after an intruder entered her apartment on October 14, 1983, awakened her with a gun to her head and a pillow over her face, and forcibly raped the frightened then-teenager in her own bed.

As the years passed, and police made no arrests, Laura feared her attacker might return. She lived in constant fear—the type of anxiety that interfered with her daily functioning. "It's really a life sentence to be raped," she says. "It's always vivid in your mind."

After the rape, Laura felt an anxiety like a "dark shadow sort of lurking near the house. For me, having everything locked and a security system was probably the best level of security I was going to get.... It's difficult to trust people or get close to people," she said. "I'm...not married. I don't have children. And you know, a lot of that has to do with letting people get close to me."

Police finally caught and arrested Laura's rapist. He was sentenced to prison for fifteen years. Laura faced him, and he apologized to her. She told him: "I have lived nineteen years of hell. And I've lived in fear because of what you did. I'm really angry about it. And I don't want to be angry anymore. Thank you for saying you're sorry and taking responsibility for it. I hope I can eventually get to the point of forgiveness."

Laura has found healing from her anxiety, and has moved on with her life. But it took her a very long time. She

---

2   H. Norman Wright, *Freedom from the Grip of Fear* (Grand Rapids: Fleming H. Revell, 2003), pp. 10-11.

has just become engaged to be married. She's determined not to be a frightened victim anymore.[3]

Life in our world today invites anxiety. Television and newspapers remind us daily of terrorist threats, drive-by shooters, car-jackers, rapists, kidnappers, and suicide bombers. You may think it's impossible to live in such a violent society and not feel anxious.

Anxieties can cause huge problems in your life. When you allow anxiety "to hide in the crevices of [your] mind: fear actually expands and grows in the darkness, exploding later with life-shattering force."[4] A constant state of anxiety will devour you, and keep you from concentrating on anything but the unhealthy fear itself. Anxiety can render you useless in God's kingdom work. It will drain your mental energy. You'll be so absorbed in fears of what might happen, you'll be unable to focus on the present moment.

"Anxiety disorders have surpassed depression and alcoholism as the number-one mental health problem in America," write Neil Anderson and Rick Miller. "We are experiencing a 'blues' epidemic in this age of anxiety, although few people will openly admit to their fears and anxieties.... Most suffer through these experiences in lonely isolation."[5]

Even mild anxiety may cause people to change daily schedules and appetite habits. They may "overload on carbohydrates, gain weight, and avoid physical activity. Some...may depend too much on alcohol, sleeping pills, other drugs, or beverages that contain caffeine." Why? "When we're consumed with dread, fear, or a sense of hopelessness, taking care of ourselves is not our

---

3   "Cry Rape," CBS Worldwide, Inc., September 19, 2003, online resource.

4   Stephen Arterburn, Paul Meier, and Robert L. Wise, *Fear Less For Life* (Nashville: Thomas Nelson Publishers, 2002), p. 26.

5   Anderson and Miller, p. 13.

number-one priority. The more we lose control over our lives, the more anxious...we grow."[6]

Anxiety, and the worry it brings, can take on a life of its own. Anxiety can make everything you do seem like a potential crisis. You may anxiously await the next possible disaster. But you don't have to keep living this way.

God's Word tells us: "Do not be anxious about anything, but in everything, by prayer and petition, with thanksgiving, present your requests to God." And then he promises: "And the peace of God, which transcends all understanding, will guard your hearts and your minds in Christ Jesus" (Phil. 4:6-7).

The Apostle Paul wrote these words to the Philippians in a time of high anxiety. Christians in the Roman Empire faced all kinds of hardships, anxieties, persecution, and even death. Life was anything but peaceful and stable for early Christians. Yet Paul still gives them this advice.

So what can we do about worry and anxiety. Pray, yes. And here are three more suggestions:

◊ Study God's Word. Scripture, as just noted, assures us that a peace beyond our human understanding will cover us, guard us, and bring comfort to our emotions and thoughts.

◊ Believe God's Word. We must believe that Scripture is God-ordained, truthful, and divinely inspired.

◊ Practice God's Word. When we put into practice the Bible's wisdom, we learn that for every "disease" of the mind and heart, Scripture gives us the answers to healing.

(Scripture addresses anxiety in other verses too, including: Ps. 55:22; Isa. 41:13; Matt. 6:25; 1 Pet. 5:7.)

---

6   Frances E. FitzGerald, "Facing the Fear Factor," Taste for Life, May 2003, p. 24.

15

Women and Phobias

A phobia 'is a constant, compulsive preoccupation with the thing, animal, or person one is afraid of.'

Dr Benjamin B. Wolman, *Children's Fears*

Phobias are intensely real to the one who suffers from them, but they are not dangerous or life-threatening. They are powerful, but they can be cured.

Listen to Annie describe her phobia—her irrational fear of non-poisonous snakes.

"I have been terrified of snakes—even non-poisonous snakes—all my life. I even react to the thought of a snake. I break out with a cold sweat, palpitating heartbeat, paralysis in my limbs, and shortness of breath. Once, when I was a teenager, I was hoeing weeds in an old pigpen. The pen was surrounded by a fence made of heavy mesh wire about five feet high. The weeds were tall, some shoulder high. Near the front of the pen was an old wooden watering trough about four feet long, turned upside down. I cut the weeds until I reached the trough, then laid my hoe down so I could turn the trough over. I reached down and casually flipped it up on one end. There, beneath the trough, was a ball of non-poisonous snakes—so many I couldn't count them. I was terrified. In desperation to get away from the snakes, I literally jumped into the fence. The impact almost knocked me down on top of the snakes.

Phobias, like the irrational fear of non-poisonous snakes, are "obsessive, compulsive, constant fears that remain one of the most powerful forces in the human psyche. Born out of the concern for self-protection, a phobia raises our apprehensions about survival to the ultimate level of self-preoccupation."

Some women are so afraid of snakes, they refuse to walk near grass, lakes, or ponds. While the fear of poisonous snakes is a healthy fear (that is, when you encounter a poisonous snake and must make a life-saving decision to fight or flee), feeling constant anxiety when no snakes are around is an unhealthy fear. If you have a snake phobia, like Annie, even seeing a picture of a snake terrifies you.

My friend Jamie recently told me that she was terrified of the ocean. When I asked her why, she replied: "It has a powerful undertow, huge waves, and dangerous animals live in it. I enjoy looking at it, but I have no desire to swim in it."

Then Jamie asked me: "Does that mean I have a phobia?"

Perhaps you are asking the same question. You might be "afraid" of high places, vicious dogs, poisonous snakes, flying in a plane, or even riding in a car. You too might wonder if you have a phobia. The Mayo Clinic answers the question like this: "Simply feeling uncomfortable or uncertain about an object or situation may be normal and common. If your phobia isn't disrupting your life, it's not considered a disorder and you may not need treatment. But if your fear becomes irrational and uncontrollable to the point that it affects your social interactions or job duties, you may have a disorder that requires medical or psychological treatment. See your doctor or mental health professional such as a psychiatrist or psychologist."[1]

Some women think they are suffering from phobias when they are really just practicing a healthy respect for something that could hurt them.

"Unhealthy fear of" and "healthy respect for" are completely different things. Healthy respect causes us to stop, take necessary precautions, and make smart life-saving decisions before we act. We should have a healthy respect for high places—gravity is a powerful force that pulls us straight down to earth. Without secure railing, and other safety measures, we could fall.

I am a dog-lover, and have two tea-cup chihuahuas I dearly adore. But you and I should have a healthy respect for dogs (and other animals with sharp teeth or claws). Dogs can be unpredictable, especially certain breeds. Dogs (as well as other animals) are capable of attacking humans, causing serious injury and even death.

We should have a healthy respect for snakes. Some types of snakes are poisonous. They can bite, and their venom can poison us.

You and I should have a healthy respect for flying in planes. Planes travel 500 miles per hour, and 30,000 feet above the earth. They can also catch fire, crash, nosedive, or explode from terrorists' bombs. We've become used to climbing into the metal tube and soaring through the skies. Showing a healthy respect for those things that can kill you is wise, not phobic.

---

1   "Phobias," MayoClinic.com, April 8, 2003.

Phobias, on the other hand, are obsessive irrational fears that can significantly interfere with social interactions and life routines. For example, they can keep highly qualified women from working the jobs they love because their offices require elevator trips to a twenty-second-floor office, and they are terrified of confined spaces (claustrophobia) and/ or heights (acrophobia). These women have three choices: they can hike up twenty-two flights of stairs; they can give in to claustrophobia and acrophobia, and change jobs; or they can get professional help to overcome this phobia that disrupts their work.

A social phobia is the overwhelming fear that you will somehow embarrass yourself in front of others. It can keep you imprisoned in your home because you are "afraid" you'll make a social blunder. If you have a social phobia, then stop and examine it for what it really is: an irrational, unfounded, unhealthy fear that can keep you from fulfilling God's purpose for your uniquely gifts, life and calling.

You can develop a phobia from any fear.[2] Some unusual phobias might tempt us to laugh, but are very real to the people who suffer them. Consider arachibutyrophobia, the fear of peanut butter sticking to your mouth; alliumphobia, the fear of garlic; pediophobia, the fear of dolls; pogonophobia, the fear of beards; zemmiphobia, the fear of the "great mole rat"; and phobophobia, the fear of fear.

Who are the people most prone to phobias? "People with phobias also tend to be more excitable, more sensitive, and more reactive to stimuli...they also are likely to be perfectionist, have a strong need for approval, a desire to be 'in control,' and suppress their feelings,

---

2   See Appendix: "A List of Common Phobias."

especially of anger and sadness. Being the victim of abuse, having overprotective parents, and growing up in a rigid household may also lead to phobias."[3]

Also know that:

Specific or special phobias are fears of things like snakes (ophidiophobia), birds (ornithophobia), cats (ailurophobia), spiders (arachnophobia), tombstones (placophobia), dirt (rupophobia), etc. They can also include fears of heights (acrophobia), empty spaces (kenophobia), lakes (limnophobia), etc.

Social phobias are fears relating to social situations, such as speaking in public (glossophobia), meeting strangers (xenophobia), being stared at (ophthalmophobia), etc.

Agoraphobia is the fear of open spaces. Actually it is much more than that. It is the terror of having another uncontrollable panic attack, especially in public. This type of phobia can keep women from ever leaving their homes.

When we examine our fears, and wonder if they are phobias, ask yourself some questions:

Are you genuinely "afraid" of things like high places, dogs, snakes, flying, etc.? Or could you possibly be using the word "afraid" when you really mean you have a "healthy respect for" high places, dogs, snakes, flying, etc.?

Does this "fear" of some thing, animal, or person interrupt your life, work, relationships, and/or worship in such a significant way that you are unable to function in everyday life?

Does your "fear" of social situations, such as meeting new people or speaking in public, keep you from going to work, church, the grocery store, or to the homes of friends?

---

3   Carol Sorgen, "Confronting Your Phobias," WebMD.aol.com, August 2, 2003.

If you suffer from a phobia, be quick to seek professional help. Don't allow a phobia to keep you from living your life with joy.

SECTION 4

FACE YOUR FEARS

16

FACE FEAR WITH GOD'S PROMISES

Have you ever counted how many references there are to fear in Scripture? Three hundred and sixty-five (one for every day of the year!). As many times as God proclaimed 'Fear not...' it is obvious that fear is a major hindrance to the Christian life. Why is it such a hindrance? Because fear is the opposite of faith.

Shannon Ethridge, *Every Woman's Battle*

I truly believe that God promises us faith when we fear tragedy. Unhealthy fears, such as tragedy, hardship, the process of dying, danger, and loss can be addressed by God's promises.

One day as Jesus preached to a large crowd, Jairus, one of the synagogue rulers, ran to him and fell at his feet. Jairus pleaded with Jesus to hurry to his house and heal his sick twelve-year-old daughter.

"My little daughter is dying," he cried. "Please come and put your hands on her so that she will be healed and live" (Mark 5:23).

Death proved a common visitor to families in ancient days. Doctors had few skills or medicines to cure the sick. Jairus felt afraid and desperate. Perhaps he considered Jesus his last hope. He had heard about this Teacher who healed the sick. He begged Jesus to follow him home.

Jesus agreed to go with him. They moved at a snail's pace, though, because crowds of people blocked their way and slowed their progress.

I can imagine frightened Jairus grabbing Jesus' arm and pulling him through the pressing people. I can imagine Jairus' anxiety and fears: "If Jesus doesn't hurry, my daughter will be dead by the time he reaches my home. Then it'll be too late for him to help her."

Then, to Jairus' further distress, Jesus stopped, looked out over the crowd, and asked: "Who touched my clothes?" (v. 30)

Jairus showed his alarm. Even Jesus' disciples stood amazed. "You see the people crowding against you," they answered, "and yet you can ask, 'Who touched me?'" (v. 31).

"Please hurry, Jesus!" Jairus might have shouted. But the Teacher didn't move. He waited. He paused without hurry until a woman emerged from the crowd and fell at his feet, trembling. Patiently, Jesus listened to her lengthy confession, the story of her twelve-year bout with continued bleeding. She told him how many doctors had tried to heal her and failed. She discussed with him her finances, the depletion of her bank account. Mark wrote that she "told him the whole truth" (v. 33). When she finished her story, Jesus blessed the woman who had suffered and bled for as long as Jairus' daughter had been alive.

"Daughter," Jesus said to the woman, "your faith has healed you. Go in peace and be freed from your suffering" (v. 34). He set her free from her fears—her fear of pain, suffering, and death.

How long did it take? A minute? An hour? Mark doesn't say. But during the conversation, "while Jesus was still speaking," some of Jairus' friends ran up to him with the tragic news: "Your daughter is dead." Then they turned to Jairus and asked: "Why bother the teacher any more?" (v. 35).

Did Jairus break down and bawl? Probably. No doubt the synagogue ruler thought: "If only Jesus hadn't stopped to heal this woman, he could have saved my daughter!"

Jesus simply turned to Jairus and said: "Don't be afraid; just believe" (v. 36).

In just a few words, Jesus told Jairus not to fear tragedy, but in the midst of misfortune, to cling to faith. "Just believe."

In the midst of our own fears, could it be that Jesus speaks to our hearts and tells us too: "Don't be afraid; just believe."

Throughout his ministry, Jesus constantly emphasized faith.

When two blind men approached Jesus and begged for healing, Jesus asked them: "Do you believe that I am able to do this?" When they said yes, Jesus touched their eyes and said: "According to your faith will it be done to you," and he restored their sight (Matt. 9:27-9).

Jesus told his disciples: "If you have faith as small as a mustard seed," you can move mountains (Matt. 17:20) and "If you have faith as small as a mustard seed, you can say to this mulberry tree, 'Be uprooted and planted in the sea,' and it will obey you" (Luke 17:6).

At one point, when faced with the weak faith of most people, Jesus wondered aloud: "When the Son of Man comes, will he find faith on the earth?" (Luke 18:8).

The apostle Paul also emphasized and encouraged faith:

"Righteousness from God comes through faith in Jesus Christ to all who believe" (Rom. 3:22). "We have been justified through faith," and "we have peace with God through our Lord Jesus Christ, through whom we have gained access by faith into this grace in which we now stand" (5:1-2). "We live by faith, not by sight" (2 Cor. 5:7). "Faith is being sure of what we hope for and certain of what we do not see" (Heb. 11:1).

Paul wrote frequently about his own faith: "I have been crucified with Christ and I no longer live, but Christ lives in me. The life I live in the body, I live by faith in the Son of God, who loved me and gave himself for me" (Gal. 2:20).

Jairus received the news of his daughter's death with great sadness. "Well, thanks anyway, Jesus," he might have said. But Jesus insisted that he, Peter, James, and John still visit Jairus' house. "It'll be a wasted trip," Jairus probably thought. When Jesus and his disciples arrived at Jarius' house, Jesus had to climb through the crowded commotion. Mourners cried and wailed loudly. Jesus simply took the dead girl by the hand and said: "Little girl, I say to you, get up!"

Immediately, the girl stood up and walked around. And, at this, Mark wrote: "They were completely astonished" (v. 42; entire story found in Mark 5:21-43).

Root yourself deeply in God's promises. Stand with confidence on your faith in Jesus Christ. Do not fear tragedy. For when, and if, tragedy comes, your faith in God will see you through it. Allow faith to give you courage. Paul's faith gave him needed courage. Faith kept him from quitting when he encountered tragedy after tragedy. Paul spoke about his faith as he prepared to "depart" this life: "I have fought the good fight," he wrote. "I have finished the race, I have kept the faith" (2 Tim. 4:7).

17

God Promises You Strength When You Fear Hardship

It is God who arms me with strength and makes my way perfect.

Psalm 18:32

I once helped out and emotionally supported a friend whose husband battled Alzheimer's. During those frightening six years before his death, her brilliant husband became a "walking dead man." He literally lost his mind. My friend lovingly took care of her husband, even when he no longer recognized her. For years, she fed him, bathed him, sang him to sleep at night, and changed his diapers. I can tell you firsthand that Alzheimer's is a terrifying disease that brings unequaled hardship to the victim as well as to the caretaker.

The hard work caused my friend serious physical exhaustion, but, at the same time, deep spiritual growth. She had little support or help from family and friends. I watched her depend on God alone as she faced each new day. She proved strong and courageous. I saw little discouragement or fear. I am convinced she received every ounce of her strength from the Lord. Her hardship reminded me of Joshua's challenge when God chose him to journey into the Promised Land after Moses' death.

"Have I not commanded you?" God asked Joshua. "Be strong and courageous. Do not be terrified; do not be discouraged, for the Lord your God will be with you wherever you go" (Josh. 1:9).

Several years ago I met an extraordinary man, Dr Robertson McQuilkin, whose wife, Muriel, then fifty-five, was diagnosed with Alzheimer's disease. Dr McQuilkin took early retirement from his prestigious and beloved profession to care full-time for Muriel. It broke his heart that Muriel slowly slipped away from him with Alzheimer's—the disease that can start so early and can torment so long. In his book, *A Promise Kept*, McQuilkin writes: "It was a slow dying for me to watch the vibrant, creative, particular person I knew and loved gradually dimming out."[1]

Each day's caring for his wife brought its share of physical and emotional hardships. Dr. McQuilkin, however, faced each one head-on. He faced and conquered each hardship as each one came to him, and he urgently sought God's strength to get through it. For years, day after day, he cared lovingly for Muriel until her death.

We need not fear hardships that may come to us. For when we face them, we can stop and remind ourselves what Jesus acknowledged in John 16:33: "In this world you will have trouble." Trouble brings hardships—death, disease, financial loss, and a host of other situations that can cause you and me to fear, and feel dreadful anxiety.

---

1   Robertson McQuilkin, *A Promise Kept* (Wheaton, ILL.: Tyndale House Publishers, Inc., 1998), p. 7.

But no matter what hardships come our way, Scripture assures us of:

> God's presence. "Do not fear, for I am with you ... I will strengthen you and help you" (Isa. 41:10).
>
> God's care. "Cast all your anxiety on him ... he cares for you" (1 Pet. 5:7).
>
> God's deliverance. "I sought the Lord ... he delivered me from all my fears" (Ps. 34:4).
>
> God's strength and peace. "The Lord gives strength to his people; the Lord blesses his people with peace" (Ps. 29:11).

"Trouble can come upon us so quickly that it catches us off guard," writes Charles Stanley. "Our immediate response may be panic, anxiety, and fear. The person of peace, however, quickly feels a power rising up inside and regaining control at the helm of his life. That power is the Holy Spirit Himself, who speaks peace to the human heart, assuring the believer, 'I'm here. I'm still in charge. Nothing is beyond My strength or My understanding. I'm with you. Don't be afraid.'"[2]

---

2   Charles Stanley, *Finding Peace* (Nashville: Thomas Nelson Publishers, 2003), pp. 27-28.

18

GOD PROMISES YOU HOPE WHEN YOU FEAR THE PROCESS OF DYING

We all have our appointed hour of death, and it will find us wherever we go. And we must be ready for it.

Dietrich Bonhoeffer, *Letters and Papers from Prison*

Most people don't like to talk about how they will die. Even fleeting thoughts of death can make them tremble with fear. The process of dying is a mystery. We, as human beings, respond with fear to those things we don't understand, or haven't yet experienced. But we know we each must take the journey of dying. No one escapes it. Scripture tells us that "there is a time for everything, and a season for every activity under heaven: a time to be born and a time to die, a time to plant and a time to uproot" (Eccles. 3:1-2). We know that one day we will die, but we still fear our anticipated death and the painful process it might include. We can be so fearful of death, in fact, we fail to live life. Dying is something the Christian need not fear. God's Word makes certain promises regarding the process of dying:

God has brought you victory over death and dying. "Death has been swallowed up in victory. Where, O death, is your victory? Where, O death is your sting?" (1 Cor. 15:54-5; see also Isa. 25:8 and Hos. 13:14)

God will comfort you in your dying and bring you relief from death and pain. "He will wipe every tear from their eyes. There will be no more death or mourning or crying or pain, for the old order of things has passed away." (Rev. 21:4)

God has destroyed death and you need not fear it. "The last enemy to be destroyed is death." (1 Cor. 15:26)

God has created you with the hope of eternity in your heart (see Eccles. 3:11). He assures you that you will be raised to life after you die physically, that you will be made alive—resurrected in Christ (1 Cor. 15:20-2). Death might be the end of physical life, but your dying is the beginning of your forever life with Christ. God has conquered death. Your dying is no longer a threat, but a promise—the assurance that you will live with Christ forever (Rom. 6:89, 23). When you face the mysterious process of dying, you are not entering into an unknown experience. Jesus himself has traveled from physical death to new life. And he has shared with you his own dying and resurrection experiences. He also has paved the way to your eternal life (John 3:12-5).

Has the thought and reality of dying troubled your heart? Are you afraid of the process, of possible pain and suffering? If so, let the Lord transform your thinking about dying. Ask him to make you a woman of hope, guiding you to rise above the common fear that dying, and the journey to new life, can bring. Know with certainty that, as a Christian, God has already prepared a place for you—and your

Christian loved ones—with him in heaven. Jesus asks us to trust him with untroubled hearts. He promises us he has gone before us to prepare for our dying and coming to him (John 14:1-4).

When I was a little girl, once or twice a year, my mother put me on a Greyhound bus headed for Rossville, Georgia, so I could visit my grandparents. (Those were the days when society proved safer for children!) She told me she had made the trip many times before. She also told me how many times the bus stopped before it reached Rossville, and the times and places of those stops. Then she assured me that when the bus stopped in Rossville, Georgia, my grandparents would be waiting for me at the station. They would meet me at the steps of the bus, and take me to their small farm homestead.

During those trips, I left my mom's arms, climbed into the bus, and looked forward to meeting my grandparents. Mom had told me precisely what I could expect during and after the long journey. I knew I'd be met by loving grandparents. I didn't worry or fear. I trusted my mother's words and experiences, and I trusted Mama and Papa to be there when I arrived.

The process of dying is no different from that bus ride to Rossville. Jesus has made the trip. He has shared with us his journey. And he has assured us that he, himself, will meet us on the other side of our dying—and bring us home.

"Death is not annihilation," writes John Claypool. "It does not represent a descent into nothingness. Death is God's way of moving us from one dwelling place into another, a journey one stage further toward God's ultimate intention for us all. If the belief in death-as-transition can take the place of death-as-annihilation, then the whole of our perspective can change."[1]

Know that you can make your unhealthy fear of dying like a weak plant with shallow roots, unable to take hold in the solid rock foundation of God's Word. For God's Word promises you, without a doubt, that you will live in eternity with him forever. You can face dying with peace and assurance, God's Word, and hope.

1   John Claypool, *Mending the Heart* (Boston: Cloister Books, 1999), p. 58.

19

GOD PROMISES YOU COURAGE WHEN YOU FEAR DANGER

The Christian's life ought to be characterized by courage, by a steadiness, a firm resolve to obey and glorify God despite all that is going on around us.

Wayne and Joshua Mack, *The Fear Factor*

Do you fear danger? Are you afraid that someone might physically hurt you? Or that a natural event, like a tornado or hurricane might cripple you? As I write this chapter, I am watching on television news the results of a terrible earthquake in Haiti. People have been killed, crushed, and lost. Buildings have crumbled—hospitals, homes, businesses. It's a sad situation made worse by the extreme poverty in the Port-au-Prince area the earthquake struck.

Danger is a reality in our world today. But, you and I must not let the threat of physical violence, or dangerous events, keep us filled with anxiety. When, and if, we face danger, we can be assured God has equipped us to face it in two distinct ways.

First, he has given us that wonderful gift of healthy fear that arms us against an enemy.

Second, God promises us his courage and protection at the moment we need it. With God's courage, you and I can deal with danger. We need not fear it.

What is courage? Courage is not fearlessness in the face of danger. Courage is accepting your fear and facing the danger in spite of it. Courage is God-given boldness to stand up to fear and overcome the enemy—whatever and whoever it may be.

David shows courage when Fear shouts, "Run away!" David stands up to the madman Goliath. And David comes out the victor.

Daniel shows courage when Fear screams, "Give in, fall down and worship this pagan King Darius, and save your life." Daniel worships God instead, and ends up facing hungry lions (Dan. 6). God closes the lions' mouths, and Daniel isn't hurt.

Esther shows courage when Fear cautions, "Let Haman destroy the Jews throughout the whole kingdom of Xerxes; just save your own neck." Esther approaches King Xerxes, risks her life, and saves her people from murder (Esther 3–8).

Martin Luther shows courage when he stands up to Emperor Charles V and the congress at Worms. Defending "the sufficiency of Scripture," Luther—his life at risk—refuses to recant his belief. "I was fearless," Luther later said. "I was afraid of nothing; God can make one so desperately bold."[1]

Scripture states clearly that we need not fear what another person can do to us. Since time began, ruthless madmen have threatened people with violence in order

---

1   Robert J. Morgan, "Here I Stand," *On This Day* (Nashville: Thomas Nelson Publishers, 1997), January 28.

to control them. Consider the world's dictators who have murdered, maimed, and terrified others to get their own way. Consider suicide-bombing terrorists who threaten violence to make the world cringe in fear, so they may pursue their own political change, make religious statements, seek revenge, etc.

"That's why people make threats. Threats have the power of fear. People know that if they can make other people afraid they can have great power over them."[2]

What does Scripture say about fearing violent people?

"But when I am afraid, I put my trust in you. O God, I praise your word. I trust in God, so why should I be afraid?" declares David when the Philistines seized him in Gath (Ps. 56:3 NLT).

"That is why we can say with confidence, 'the Lord is my helper, so I will not be afraid. What can mere mortals do to me?'" (Heb. 13:6 NLT).

Consider the following assurances from the Psalms—such beautiful words of hope and encouragement for all of us. Each affirms with confidence God's presence in your life when you encounter chaos and fear danger.

Psalm 46:1-3: "God is our refuge and strength, an ever-present help in trouble. Therefore we will not fear, though the earth give way and the mountains fall into the heart of the sea, though its water roar and foam and the mountains quake with their surging."

Psalm 91:4-6: "He will cover you with his feathers, and under his wings you will find refuge; his faithfulness will be your shield and rampart. You will not fear the terror of night, nor the arrow that flies by day, nor the

---

2   Wayne and Joshua Mack, *The Fear Factor* (Tulsa: Hensley Publishing, 2002), p. 56.

pestilence that stalks in the darkness, nor the plague that destroys at midday."

Psalm 91:11-12: "For he will command his angels concerning you to guard you in all your ways; they will lift you up in their hands, so that you will not strike your foot against a stone."

Psalm 121:7-8: "The Lord will keep you from all harm—he will watch over your life; the Lord will watch over your coming and going both now and forevermore."

God's promises!

Perhaps you face danger each day. Maybe you live and/or work in the inner city or on a dangerous mission field in a foreign country. Daily you must be on guard and mentally armed to protect yourself from very possible harm—drive-by shooters, violent gang members, thieves, and car-jackers. I too have lived and worked in the middle of a violent inner city. I memorized the Bible verses that I've included in this chapter, and recited them as I walked dangerous streets and when I found myself in scary places with sadistic people. I dug my roots down deep in God's Word when he planted me in a place that might have otherwise created constant terror in my heart. I depended on him, his Word, and his promises to keep me from harm. And, through his grace, he did.

Maybe you serve your country in the armed forces. As I write this chapter, the United States is still engulfed in the Iraqi War. Men and women are protecting our country by offering their lives and skills to that war effort. Many of them have already come home in body bags. Every day brings fear to those in active combat in Iraq. They cannot, for one second, let down their guard and relax or rest.

My dad served in World War II. When he died, back in 1999, my mother gave me his World War II military-issued Bible. It included the New Testament and Psalms. It is bent, crumpled, and water damaged, but intact. The inside flyleaf reads: Robert C. Wyse, Fort Pierce, Florida, August 7, 1944. At that time, my father was only seventeen years old! He enlisted, and somehow made them believe he was older.

Beside his name reads the military directive: "By special request of the U.S. Military and Naval Authorities you are instructed to place your NAME ONLY on the fly leaf, nothing more. On no account name your organization, post, ship or station at any place in this book. To do so might afford valuable information to the enemy."

The first page of the Bible contains a letter from the White House, dated January 25, 1941. It reads: "As commander-in-Chief I take pleasure in commending the reading of the Bible to all who serve in the armed forces of the United States. Throughout the centuries, men of many faiths and diverse origins have found in the Sacred Book words of wisdom, counsel and inspiration. It is a fountain of strength and now, as always, an aid in attaining the highest aspirations of the human soul. Very sincerely yours, Franklin D. Roosevelt."

As my dad faced danger each day during his service, he had within his hands this Bible, and within the Bible, this prayer for safety: "Our Father, which art in heaven, I bow reverently to ask that Thou wilt...keep me strong, fearless and faithful ever to my Country and to Thee. And, dear Heavenly Father, I pray especially: that Thou wilt watch over, protect and guard, during my absence from home, those whom I love. In Jesus name I pray. Amen."[3]

---

3   "The Prayer of a Bluejacket," The Gideons, International (Philadelphia: National Publishing Company, 1943.

As I hold this small, worn Bible in my hands, I wonder how many times, in the face of danger, my dad, as a teenager, pulled the Bible from his pocket and prayed this prayer. How many times did he turn to the Psalms and pray the prayers of David?

"The Lord is my light and my salvation—whom shall I fear? The Lord is the stronghold of my life—of whom shall I be afraid... Though an army besiege me, my heart will not fear" (Ps. 27:1).

"You are my hiding place. You will protect me from trouble and surround me with songs of deliverance" (Ps. 32:7).

20

God Promises You Comfort When You Fear Loss

The righteous cry out, and the Lord hears them; he delivers them from all their troubles. The Lord is close to the brokenhearted and saves those who are crushed in spirit.

Psalm 34:17-18

Do you fear rejection? Are you afraid people won't like you? Some women desperately want intimacy, yet they fear rejection from someone they love. They know that marriage, and even friendship, involves vulnerability. Yet they are afraid to risk hurt, embarrassment, or abandonment.

Sometimes a woman chooses to risk rejection, and she allows herself to become vulnerable. She meets a man and falls in love. Regardless of her fears, she gives herself completely to him in marriage. Then the worst happens. Her husband abandons her. He divorces her. At that moment, she discovers what numerous women before her have already discovered: No one can hurt you as much as someone you love, someone with whom you've shared vulnerable intimacy, someone you've promised in marriage to spend the rest of your life.

"Intimate relationships bring up our most potent fears because it is there that we feel the most vulnerable. We may function at a high level in the rest of our lives, only to turn to jelly at any rejection or perceived rejection by a partner."[1]

Lisa is a Christian woman who risked rejection and vulnerability when she married Steve. She loved Steve. For the first time in her life, Steve made her feel like a valuable human being. He affirmed her. Having little self-esteem, Lisa thought Steve gave her worth and significance. She based her whole identity and self-confidence on him. Shortly after she married, however, some old fears resurfaced. She worried that Steve would stop loving her, that she might one day be alone again, that she might not have a husband to love and cherish her. Day by day, her fears grew.

Then one day, her worst nightmare came true. Her husband told her he no longer loved her. He wanted a divorce. After the divorce, Lisa felt lost. Worthless. She felt anxious about the future. Rejection by her husband seemed more than she could bear.

"I was so crippled by the fear of the unknown, rejection, loneliness, loss of control, and feelings of worthlessness," Lisa admitted, "that one day I could not bear the burden anymore. I was driving home from work one afternoon, and was stopped at a railroad crossing. The train went racing by, and I let my foot off the brake. I inched my way up to the railroad track, inch-by-inch, closer and closer, until I could feel the vibration of the train moving my car."

---

1   Susan Forward, *Emotional Blackmail* (New York: HarperCollins, 1997), p. 43.

Lisa stopped and thought about what she planned to do. Then, in desperation, she cried out to God. "Help me, Lord! Help me!" Then she heard an inner voice speak to her heart. "Be still, be still."

"A few moments passed and the train was gone," she says. "The bells stopped ringing and the lights stopped flashing."

That's the moment God gave Lisa comfort and understanding. For a long time she wondered about the meaning of the inner voice that told her to "be still, be still." One day, as she read Scripture, she discovered Psalm 46:10: "Be still, and know that I am God." In his own way, in his perfect timing, God reminded Lisa to take time to be reminded of his love for her.

When Lisa now thinks about her moment of despair at the railroad crossing, she reflects: "I was not only at a railroad crossing, I was at a life crossing. I knew the journey was not going to be easy. But I knew I had to choose which path I was going to take."

Lisa chose life and faith over fear and despair. She put herself in God's hands. She chose to believe God's promises. She decided to stop demanding that her "own will" be done, and she asked God that "his will" be done in her life.

"Why did I fear these things?" she now asks. "Because I followed my own will and not God's will for me. God clearly says he is going to take care of me, but when I do not seek his face, I do not see the comfort he is willing to provide."

Yes, Lisa, God will take care of you. He will comfort you. And he will comfort every fearful woman who surrenders her life and her will to him.

Are you afraid of losing someone or something you love? God promises you comfort if you fear loss. Listen to the affirming words written by the psalmist, David:

"I have set the Lord always before me. Because he is at my right hand, I will not be shaken" (Ps. 16:8).

"Where can I go from your Spirit? Where can I flee from your presence? If I go up to the heavens, you are there; if I make my bed in the depths, you are there. If I rise on the wings of the dawn, if I settle on the far side of the sea, even there your hand will guide me, your right hand will hold me fast" (Ps. 139:7-10).

"Even though I walk through the valley of the shadow of death, I will fear no evil, for you are with me; your rod and your staff, they comfort me" (Ps. 23:4).

When you fear any kind of loss—whether divorce, death of a loved one, financial upset, loss of employment, or loss of health—you can find deep peaceful comfort in the loving promises of Jesus: "Peace I leave with you; my peace I give you. I do not give to you as the world gives. Do not let your hearts be troubled and do not be afraid" (John 14:27).

You can know with certainty that whatever anxious situation you face, you are rooted in the firm foundation of faith. Faith in God will sustain you no matter what threatens to break your heart and crush your spirit.

"Probably the thing I fear most is the loss (death) of those close to my heart," admits my friend Janice. "I think the basis of that fear is the loneliness and loss I would feel—the abandonment."

"This fear arose in me following the death of my mother over twelve years ago," she remembers. "It surges and wanes from time to time, partly I think with my emotional ups and downs."

How does Janice deal with this fear? "The one thing I have found effective in dealing with and conquering this fear has been my faith," she says. "Whenever I feel this fear welling up, I find that devoting intentional time to Scripture study and prayer helps me put things back into perspective. Ultimately I know God is sufficient for my every need, and he will sustain me through any such loss. I know he loves me, and he wants only what is best for me within his purposes. Nevertheless, sometimes I need to take time and let him remind me of those things in new and deeper ways."

SECTION 5

CONQUER YOUR FEARS WITH CHRIST'S EXAMPLE

21

CONQUER FEAR OF EVIL WITH CHRIST'S WORDS

Your enemy the devil prowls around like a roaring lion looking for someone to devour. Resist him, standing firm in the faith.

1 Peter 5:8-9

Do you fear the Evil One, the one who stalks you like a roaring lion? Early Christians were often fed to hungry lions. Recently I stood inside the Coliseum in Rome and just imagined the horrible events that once took place there. Christians, criminals, and other people endured lions (and other wild animals) attacking and killing them, then devouring their bodies. People in the stands watched gladiators mutilate and murder one another. They watched for fun, entertainment – a sporting event for up to 70,000 Romans at one time.

The Psalmist speaks of people who intentionally hurt others when he writes: "Like lions they crouch silently, waiting to pounce on the helpless. Like hunters they capture their victims and drag them away in nets. The helpless are overwhelmed and collapse; they fall beneath the strength of the wicked" (Ps. 10:8-10 NLT).

How interesting that Peter compares Satan to a lion. Lions are known as "fearless" and the "king of beasts." They have powerful bodies, large heads, and a fierce loud roar. They can grow up to forty-five inches high, more than nine feet long, and weigh more than 500 pounds. In Jesus' day, lions were common, and lived in eastern Europe (as far north as Romania), in southern and southwestern Asia, and throughout Africa. President Theodore Roosevelt ranked the lion as a "hunter's most dangerous opponent." Often a bullet in its heart won't keep a lion from charging and killing a hunter.[1]

I emphasize the fear of evil in its own special category, because we are all so surrounded by evil in our world today. I don't understand how a human being can purposely hurt another human being, yet it happens all the time. I also emphasize the fear of evil because Jesus dealt so often with evil, and the Evil One. He knew the fear and danger the Evil One caused. He encountered numerous demon-possessed people in his travels and ministry. He usually drove out the demons and restored the person. Matthew writes: "When evening came, many who were demon-possessed were brought to him, and he drove out the spirits with a word and healed all the sick" (Matt. 8:16).

The Bible cites references to Satan and his evil from Genesis to Revelation. Scripture states that Satan continues to reign as the god of this age (2 Cor. 4:4), even though at the cross Christ triumphed over Satan's power (Col. 2:15). He causes continued conflict with humans (Eph. 6:11-18), and works at tempting and accusing them (1 Cor. 5:5; 1 John 5:16; Rev. 12:10). Scripture assures us,

---

1   *The World Book Encyclopedia, Vol. 11* (Chicago: Field Enterprises Educational Corp., 1963), pp. 298-301.

however, that Satan and evil will be ousted from heaven (Rev. 12:7-12), as well as from earth (Rev. 5:1-19:16).

Satan and his force of demons are powerful in the world today. We see evidence everywhere of the evil and havoc they wreak. But should you and I, as Christian women, be afraid of the Evil One? Scripture tells us no. Why?

Jesus claims he is more powerful than evil and the Evil One (see 1 John 4:4; Rev. 20:2). God's power over Satan can set your mind at rest when you are tempted to fear evil and Satan's limited strength. Evil cannot defeat God. As a member of his beloved family, God protects you from the Evil One. You can meet and face life like the small child who walks past the school bullies with his own personal muscular bodyguard. No bully can match your Bodyguard's strength and power. You can saunter confidently and unafraid. John 17:15 assures you that Jesus prays for your protection, just as he prayed for the protection of his disciples when he said: "My prayer is not that you take them out of the world but that you protect them from the evil one." You can know that Jesus' prayers "cover" you each second of your entire life. Scripture tells you and me not to fear Satan, but to get rid of him. How? "Resist him, standing firm in the faith" (1 Pet. 5:9).

Jesus shows, by his own example, how to deal with evil, fear, and temptation (in Matt. 4:1-11). After John baptized Jesus, the Lord headed to the wilderness to pray. The wilderness was a scary place to be alone. It is an uninhabited wasteland infested with poisonous snakes, scorpions, and wild animals. Jewish tradition in Jesus' day regarded it as a home for demons, a place of darkness (Jer. 2:6, 31), and a place "cut off from life" (Lev. 16:22). It was here that Satan came to Jesus to frighten and tempt him. But each time Satan spoke, Jesus shot back with words from Scripture.

◊ First temptation: Satan: "If you are the Son of God, tell these stones to become bread." Jesus: "No! The Scriptures say, 'People need more than bread for their life; they must feed on every word of God.'" (Remember, Jesus was famished—he had not eaten in four days.)

◊ Second temptation: Satan: "If you are the Son of God, throw yourself down [from the highest point of the temple].' Jesus: "It is also written: 'Do not put the Lord your God to the test.'"

◊ Third temptation: Satan: "All this I will give you [all the kingdoms of the world], if you will bow down and worship me." Jesus: "Away from me, Satan! For it is written: 'Worship the Lord your God, and serve him only.'"

"Then the devil left him," Matthew writes, "and angels came and attended him."

You too can be rid of the Evil One, and you have a Father to protect you from him. Jesus answered Satan's scare tactics and temptations just as you and I must stand up to Satan today: with God's Word. Growing deep roots in his Word will keep evil at bay. Whenever Satan tempts you to fear him, echo the words of Jesus—out loud: "Away from me, Satan!...for it is written...."

22

CONQUER FEAR OF HATE WITH CHRIST'S LOVE

But I say, love your enemies! Pray for those who persecute you! In that way, you will be acting as true children of your Father in heaven.

Jesus, Matthew 5:44-5 NLT

Like evil, hate also deserves individual attention. Jesus often encountered hate. Even in our time, hate, and hate-induced crimes, can cause us to live our lives in fear.

In Jesus' day, hate proved just as intense as in our own day. Jesus confronted and conquered hate's fears with love. Time and again, Christ's love transformed human hate. Just as we must face evil (and the Evil One) with Christ's words, we must face hate, and the fear it causes, with Christ's love. Fear and hate melt in the face of love.

Let's look more closely at Christ's love. How beautifully Paul describes love! He says that love is patient, kind, protective, and trusting. It doesn't envy or boast, it is not proud or rude. Love is giving, not self-seeking. It's not easily angered and keeps no record of wrongs. Love forgives. It doesn't hold a grudge. Love rejoices with the truth. Love hopes, perseveres, and never fails. Of the three things that will forever remain: faith, hope, and love—the greatest of these is love (see 1 Cor. 13).

I grew up in the Southern United States surrounded by hate—racial hate. Racial hatred caused me much fear as a young girl in Atlanta, Georgia, during the civil rights era when Dr. Martin Luther King, Jr., marched for peace and renounced bigotry and hatred. The very air seemed to harbor hate, and people breathed it in and out twenty-four hours a day. I remember the public water fountains and the restrooms marked "for coloreds" and "for whites only." I watched the evening news and saw the fear and violence racial hatred produced. During church on Sunday mornings, we learned to "love our neighbor." But after the worship service, my family and other church families ate at Lester Maddox's famous restaurant, "The Pickrick." While I waited in long lines to order my food, I overheard the prejudiced jokes about African-Americans. I heard the loud, hateful laughter that followed. I heard the racial slurs pour from the beak of Maddox's old black myna bird that entertained the customers in line. I saw the "souvenir ax handles" Maddox sold in his restaurant. They came in different sizes—in order to "beat" black people of different ages—from children to adults. Fear and hate had been built into the very fabric of Southern culture in the United States. We didn't think much about our un-Christian racial prejudice during those days. It's just "the way it was." It confused me, and I could never understand it, even as a child.

I weathered society's storm of racial hatred throughout my childhood and teens. I now live in Birmingham, Alabama, the site of much of the civil unrest during those years. Prior to 1963, the then-deeply segregated steel capital of the South—Birmingham—showed the whole world the ugliness of racial hate and fear. (It had been nicknamed "Bombingham" because of the frequent Klan

128

bombings in that city.) The city also showed that the power of Christ's self-giving love can conquer the most despicable inhumanity. But it cost the lives of four girls and two boys, as well as many others.

One Sunday morning, September 15, 1963, four little African-American girls dressed up in their frilly white Sunday school dresses. They walked into Birmingham's Sixteenth Street Baptist Church to worship God on Youth Sunday. They didn't know that a Klan bomb had been planted beside the church. That morning, they all died in an explosion. A 1963 reporter from the *Birmingham World* wrote: "Their bodies were stacked up on top of each other like bales of hay from the crumbling ruins left by the dynamiting ... They were girls. They were children. They were members of the Negro group, they were victims of cruel madness, ... vile bigotry and deadly hate.[1]

I vividly remember the event primarily because I was the same age, and had the same name—Denise—as one of the girls, Denise McNair.

Birmingham's Carolyn McKinstry, an African-American youth in the church that Sunday in 1963, barely survived that bombing. Only minutes before the bomb exploded, she stopped by the restroom and spoke to her four friends. The blast rocked the church building, broke the windows, and killed Denise McNair, Addie Collins, Cynthia Wesley, and Carole Robertson. Addie's sister, Sarah, stood in another part of the restroom that morning. The blast injured her, and blinded one eye.

Since then, Carolyn has spent her lifetime working to eliminate racial hate and promote love and peace.

---

1   "Killers of the Innocents," *Birmingham World*, September 18, 1963.

That evening, on September 15, 1963, as "all Birmingham waited with taut nerves...for a possible major eruption of racial violence,"[2] Mayor Albert Boutwell begged people to stay home. But, later that night, two more African-American children were senselessly killed: Virgil Ware, thirteen, and Johnnie Robinson, sixteen. Two white youths—both sixteen and Eagle Scouts—murdered Virgil Ware as he rode his bike down the street. A white policeman shot and killed Johnnie Robinson for throwing rocks at cars driven by white people.

At Johnnie's funeral, the Reverend A. L. Woods said: "Not only are we here for the funeral of Johnnie Robinson, but I think we can say we are here for the funeral of Birmingham."[3]

Fortunately, the minister's words proved not to be prophetic. The church bombing served as a wake-up call to the entire city—and world! Immediately, Christians of all races and denominations rallied together to face Birmingham's fear-caused hatred. Slowly but surely they dashed hate as they gave the city a healthy dose of Christ's love.

Today, Birmingham, Alabama, is a delightful place to live, for many different races. It has been transformed into a world-class medical center with African Americans serving in medicine, business, industry, education, and politics.

You and I have both seen how hate causes fear. But Christ's love conquers hate. When you experience fear caused by hate, face it with Christ's love. His love dissolves fear, and turns hate into hope. Surely, the "mark of Jesus" is love.

---

2   Arthur Osgood, "Racial Tension Mounts in Birmingham After Four Killed in Church Bombing," *The Montgomery Advertiser*, September 16, 1963.

3   Robert Gordon, "Birmingham Pays Homage to Slain Teenage Boys," *Birmingham World*, September 25, 1963.

23

CONQUER FEAR OF CRUELTY WITH CHRIST'S FORGIVENESS

Bear with each other and forgive whatever grievances you may have against one another. Forgive as the Lord forgave you.

Colossians 3:13

Evil, hate, and cruelty have been lasting marks of civilization since time began. Not a day goes by that we fail to hear of the worldwide fears caused by evil, hate, and cruelty. I've given "cruelty" its own emphasis in this chapter. Cruelty causes humans to cringe with fear.

Have you ever experienced a person's cruelty? I have. We don't live long in this world without experiencing cruelty and the fear it causes. It does not seem possible that God calls us to forgive people who cause us painful and needless cruelty. But he does. When the worst happens—when cruel people hurt us, and hurt those we love, Christ calls us to do the illogical, the unnatural, the unbelievable—he counsels us to forgive them. You see, cruelty loses its power to cause us fear when we challenge it with forgiveness.

Beth Nimo and Darrell Scott know about fear caused by cruelty. On April 20, 1999, their daughter, Rachel Scott, was shot to death as she ate lunch with her friends at school. Rachel, seventeen, a devoted Christian, was one of thirteen people killed at Columbine High School in Littleton, Colorado. Her classmates, Eric Harris and Dylan Klebold, walked through the high school halls, made racial remarks, and coldly shot their fellow students. The shots from those guns pierced the soul of a nation. It made people sob and shudder with fear.

The killers shot Rachel twice in her legs and once in her torso. Rachel tried to crawl away from her attackers. She sought safety. Her shooters walked away, but returned only seconds later. Harris grabbed Rachel by her hair, jerked her head up, and shouted a question in her face: "Do you believe in God?" When she said she did, Harris shot her in the head.

Rachel's parents confessed they felt angry and sad when their daughter was killed. Who wouldn't feel that way?! But they also wanted to forgive their daughter's killers.

"That is probably one of the most difficult issues to face when you have been so deeply wronged," they write in their book, *Rachel's Tears*. "Our understanding of God's heart left us only one choice, the decision to forgive. It was the choice of Jesus as He hung on a cross dying....If we do not forgive, we end up in perpetual anger and bitterness and eventually offend others with our words or actions. If we forgive, we experience a 'letting go' or cleansing process that frees us from the offender."[1]

Forgiveness, however, did not happen overnight. The pain remained fresh for a long time. When *Time* magazine later wrote a cover story on the Columbine killings, Beth

---

1   Beth Nimmo and Darrell Scott, *Rachel's Tears* (Nashville: Thomas Nelson, 2000) xxii.

cried for weeks. She felt a huge amount of anger and personal hurt when she read that Rachel had been on the killers' target list. Beth struggled with being "very unforgiving and very bitter." She confesses that "the more knowledge I had about the two boys, the more violated I felt, and the more grace it took for me to walk in forgiveness."[2]

A year after Rachel's death, her parents still struggle with forgiving Eric and Dylan. Forgiveness has been a daily battle for Beth. "From the beginning I have asked the Lord to give me real forgiveness for Eric and Dylan, but that desire is repeatedly tested," she admits.[3]

Rachel's parents faced Eric and Dylan's cruelty with Christ's forgiveness, just as they believed God's Word teaches Christians to do.

"Our hearts...could not have harbored un-forgiveness," they agreed. "Un-forgiveness blocks God's ability to flow through us to help others."[4]

Have you encountered fear from the cruel hand of another? If so, face and fight your fear with forgiveness, for forgiveness will free you from fear. Forgiveness is not a "feeling," but a choice you make with God's help. Of course, it's not easy. And it may take a long time. But forgiveness remains the only way to conquer the fears caused by cruelty.

---

2   Ibid., pp. 171-2.

3   Ibid., p. 171.

4   Ibid., p. xxiii.

24

CONQUER FEAR OF FEAR WITH CHRIST'S COURAGE

You gain strength, courage, and confidence by every experience in which you really stop to look fear in the face. You must do the thing which you think you cannot do.

Anna Eleanor Roosevelt

Agoraphobia also deserves its own category and chapter. Agoraphobia has two meanings: the fear of open places, and the fear of fear itself.

The fear of open places can keep a woman trembling inside her bedroom, and afraid to leave her house. She may live that way for months, and even years, never venturing past her front door.

The fear of fear itself is what President Franklin Delano Roosevelt, in his March 4, 1933, Inaugural Address, spoke about when he told the frightened American people: "The only thing we have to fear is fear itself—nameless, unreasoning, unjustified terror which paralyzes needed efforts to convert retreat into advance."

Some women fear fear. It's a constant battle they fight. They go out of their way to avoid all situations, people, and places that threaten to produce the feelings of fear.

They worry that fear will cause them to react in unsociable ways, and that they may embarrass themselves in front of those they most want to impress. They aren't sure they can adequately handle their behavior when it is controlled and influenced by fear.

"I'm not afraid of speaking publicly," a woman once told me. "I have no problem articulating well what I want to say. But I'm afraid I'll appear to be afraid. When I step up in front of a crowd, I'm worried my knees will knock, my face will break out in a sweat, and my voice will quiver. I'm afraid of looking like I'm afraid!"

Rather than speak up and express her opinion or state her beliefs, this woman remains seated, quiet, and verbally uninvolved. What does it matter if this woman looks like she is afraid, if her knees knock together, her face sweats, and her voice quivers? The purpose in speaking publicly is to get a message across to other people, not to be admired as a successful, polished speaker. It's communication—not a contest.

Another woman confessed to me that she prefers to stay at home because she fears getting lost in the city. "I'm afraid I'll get turned around and wander down some unknown street, and panic because I feel lost and afraid." Her worry about becoming afraid keeps her bound to her familiar neighborhood, and prevents her from making wonderful new discoveries. Perhaps with a good map of the city, a hand-held GPS system, or the presence of a friend who knows the area, this woman could bring her fears under control.

One woman admitted to me she is fearful of having a panic attack in public—that she doesn't want to leave her house, visit her friends, or go to work anymore. Fear has choked out everything this woman holds dear. She is afraid to go anywhere that might prevent a quick escape lest she suddenly have feelings of panic.

Agoraphobics (those who fear fear itself, as well as those who fear "the marketplace" or "open spaces") think about fear all the time. They are consumed by it. It imprisons them. When agoraphobia becomes disabling, a woman needs professional help. She cannot help herself, but needs a mental health worker or Christian counselor to encourage, teach, and support her. Time after time, women with agoraphobia have received professional help, and have known courage and freedom from their fears.

Agoraphobia can also keep a woman from living up to her potential as a worker and witness in God's kingdom. It can keep women from serving God and fulfilling their sense of calling. "Fear causes us to run away from things that frighten us. And fear becomes sinful when it causes us to run away from the things God has commanded us to do."[1]

The Bible tells two interesting stories of people who allowed fear to deter them from their mission and purpose. My favorite is of Joshua and Caleb and the other ten spies (see Num. 13:1-14:38; Deut. 1:36; Josh. 14:6; 15:19). When the spies returned from their fact-finding mission to the Promised Land of Canaan, they all reported to Moses that the land produced abundant fruit, and flowed with milk and honey. That was the good news. But ten of the spies also said they could not conquer the land, that they seemed like grasshoppers compared to the huge people who lived there. In other words, they were afraid. That was the bad news. And who could blame them?

---

1   Wayne and Joshua Mack, *The Fear Factor* (Tulsa: Hensley Publishing, 2002), p. 55.

That's when courageous Caleb spoke up: "We should go up and take possession of the land," he said, "for we can certainly do it." Joshua agreed with him. "If the Lord is pleased with us, he will lead us into that land...and will give it to us...the Lord is with us. Do not be afraid of them." Their brave words upset the people, and they rose up to stone Joshua and Caleb. But the two men believed in God, and were not afraid to put their faith into action. God rewarded their bravery and belief by allowing them alone to enter the Promised Land.

In the second story, Jesus tells about a servant, who like the ten spies, suffered from the fear of fear. A master had three servants. Before he embarked on a journey, he entrusted gifts of money (talents) to each one (Matt. 25:14-30). To one servant, wise and fearless, he gave $5,000. To another servant, somewhat courageous and somewhat wise, he gave $2,000. To the last servant, a man controlled by fear, he gave only $1,000. This servant was so afraid of losing the money and disappointing his master, he failed to invest it. He simply dug a hole in the ground and hid it. The fear of fear paralyzed him and kept him from producing any financial gain or interest on the money.

When the master returned home, he asked each servant how much profit his money had produced. The servant responsible for $5,000 gave the owner $10,000. He had invested with great wisdom and courage, and had doubled the money. The servant responsible for $2,000 gave the owner $4,000. He too had managed to double the money.

"Good job!" the master said to the brave, industrious servants.

The servant responsible for $1,000, however, returned to the owner the original $1,000. Then he stuttered: "Master,

I knew that you are a hard man...so I was afraid and went out and hid your talent in the ground" (vv. 24-5).

I can sympathize with the servant whose fear provoked him to avoid risk—losing the entire $1,000. He probably feared harsh words from his master if he lost the money, so he "froze with fear" and buried it. But, as we see, his inaction didn't help him. He still received harsh words from his master.

"You wicked, lazy servant!" the owner replied. "You should have put my money on deposit with the bankers, so that when I returned I would have received it back with interest." Then he commanded servants to "take the talent from him and give it to the one who has the ten talents" (vv. 26-8).

Many things in life can cause us to freeze up, fear the outcome, and fail to take a risk, even a slight risk. What must we do during these times?

We must depend on Christ to give us courage.

We must reach up to God and study his Word. "The root of any phobia is a belief that is not based in truth. These false beliefs need to be uprooted and replaced by the truth of God's Word."[2]

We must trust God, believe his Word, and put it into action.

We must, at times, seek out Christian friends and church leaders to help us face, fight, and conquer our fears.

And when our fears interfere with our daily life, work, and family responsibilities, we must enlist the professional help of a trained Christian counselor and/or mental health personnel.

---

2   Neil T. Anderson and Rich Miller, *Freedom from Fear* (Eugene, OR: Harvest House, 1999), p. 198.

It takes courage to face our fears, but Christ gives us the needed courage. We can find help, and we can be rid of those fears that obstruct our lives.

25

CONQUER FEAR OF SUFFERING WITH CHRIST'S ACCEPTANCE

I tell you the truth, unless a kernel of wheat falls to the ground and dies, it remains only a single seed. But if it dies, it produces many seeds."

Jesus, John 12:24

Death, and the fear of dying and suffering, can be a frightening part of most women's lives. Because of this, I have given it special emphasis and extra space in this book. I've talked with many Christian women about death. Some greatly fear death, but have come to accept death as a part of life. They are certain they will be with God when they die, and that gives them confidence and courage. But almost every Christian woman I interviewed candidly admitted she greatly fears the possible suffering that dying may bring her. I heard the following answer from the majority of women I interviewed:

"It's not the death or the dying that is the problem, but how it happens and the suffering it might bring. To be trapped in a body, not able to communicate, sick and in pain for a long time, would be the worst. That's what most scares me," they said.

The suffering caused by dying is a common concern for most people. Jesus himself feared the suffering his death would inevitably bring. He dreaded the piercing pain of scourging and crucifixion. Remember that Jesus, the Word, was made flesh and thus suffered the sensation of pain (see John 1:1-2, 14). Before his arrest and crucifixion, Jesus considered his upcoming suffering and it caused him to pray in anguish: "Father, if you are willing, take this cup [crucifixion] from me" (Luke 22:42). He prayed with such agony "his sweat was like drops of blood falling to the ground" (v. 44). Three times he prayed earnestly, begging God to spare him the painful process of suffering on a cross. "My soul is overwhelmed with sorrow to the point of death," he told his disciples (Mark 14:34). "Everything is possible for you," he told his Father. "Take this cup from me" (v. 36). But the fear of suffering didn't deter Jesus from accepting God's will and accomplishing God's work—the salvation of humanity. "Yet not what I will, but what you will," he finally prayed, and with complete acceptance, he surrendered himself, and his fear of pain, to God's will.

In 1623, John Donne suffered a near-fatal illness. The clergyman lay in his bed stricken with Black Plague—the disease that killed thousands all around him. As he waited for death, he listened to London's church bells ring out and announce another person's death. He thought "for whom the bell tolled" would soon be for him. While he suffered and waited to die, he prayed and reflected. He surrendered himself to dying with this prayer to God: "Your son [Jesus] felt a sadness in his soul unto death," Donne prayed, "and a reluctance, even fear, as that hour approached. But he had an antidote too: 'Yet not my will, but thine be done.'"...

When your Son cried out 'My God, my God, why hast thou forsaken me?' you reached out your hand not to heal his sad soul, but to receive his holy soul. Neither did he desire to hold it from you, but surrendered it to you."[1]

Let me ask you to stop here for a moment and read John 11:1-44. Now that you've read the passage, let's have an imaginary conversation with Lazarus—the man Jesus raised from death. Let's pretend it goes something like this:

"Lazarus," we ask. "What was dying like?'

"Peace!" he answers. "My death brought me peace, as God himself enveloped me within his loving arms. And joy," he adds. "Greater joy than I could've ever imagined on Earth."

"You are fortunate, Lazarus," we tell him. "You are one of the few people Jesus raised from the dead. He gave you the opportunity to come back, to live again with your sisters, to enjoy life."

"Why do you call me 'fortunate'?" Lazarus asks. "I was snatched from the loving arms of God, and brought back to the pain and suffering of life! Do you think I wanted to come back? Of course not! I wanted to stay at home with my Father. I was more alive with my heavenly Father than I could ever be here on Earth."

"But Lazarus," we say, "Jesus gave you the 'gift of life.'"

"From your experience," Lazarus responds, "you can see only the 'gift of life.' After you die, after you are embraced by God, your perspective will greatly change. You will no longer see human life as 'gift.' You will understand that death itself is the 'gift' of God. For the believer in Christ, death is not the end of life. Death is the beginning of life! It's like being born—all over again!"

---

1   Philip Yancey, "Thanksgiving in the Midst of Fear," *Christianity Today International/ Christian History* magazine, 2003, online source.

"Death is like 'being born'?" we ask.

"Of course it is!" exclaims Lazarus. "Consider an unborn baby. The baby feels safe and secure within her mother's womb. She is happy. She doesn't want to leave her cozy, familiar nest. But then the baby experiences birth. She leaves her mother, and she enters a bright new world—a world she could never before have imagined within the walls of the womb. That's what death is like. I wish I could tell you the depth of peace, joy, and love that waits for you in the Father's arms!"

"And think about this," Lazarus tells us. "I had to die a second time. I experienced another sickness and suffering and death, another funeral. You ask me if I would choose to come back from death to life the first time I died? No. Never. Even though death often involves suffering, death is a gift if Jesus is your Lord."

Does this imaginary dialogue with Lazarus surprise you? Did you imagine before your "conversation" with him that the resurrected Lazarus walked from his tomb, joyfully shed his funeral clothes, happily beat on his chest, and thanked Jesus for a life restored? Did you ever consider that Lazarus might not have wanted to come back to life? That Lazarus may have wanted to curse Jesus, not thank him? Could it be that "Jesus wept" over Lazarus' tomb, not because he mourned his friend's death, but because he knew Lazarus must be raised again to the pain of life on Earth (see John 11:35)?

And can you imagine Lazarus living each day, yearning for the gift of death—the moment he could finally go Home, climb back into the Father's lap, and be embraced by pure unconditional love?

John Claypool writes: "There is...good reason to believe that what happens to us at the end of our lives in history is akin to what happens to us at the beginning; namely, we die to a smaller place that we might move on to a great."[2]

Dying—and even the suffering that might accompany it—need not be dreaded. You and I can face dying like Jesus did—with acceptance. Yes, we might endure pain in the process, but, as believers in Jesus Christ, we will not face suffering alone. God's Word assures us that God will hold us in his great love—in living and in dying.

"God's love for us accompanies us through every stage—from sperm and egg to fetus and infant, then the child, the adolescent, and from there to maturity and old age."[3]

Know that, as a Christian, you are a woman of great strength. You have the ability to face your fear of dying—whether you fear the end of your existence on Earth or the suffering it might include. You can stand strong, with courage and valor, because the Holy Spirit—the Helper, the Comforter—lives within you.

---

2   John Claypool, *Mending the Heart* (Boston: Cloister Books, 1999), p. 59.

3   Ibid.

SECTION 6

TESTIMONIES OF FEARS CONQUERED

26

OLD TESTAMENT HEROES
WE SHOULD ALL KNOW ABOUT

I was forty years old when Moses the servant of the Lord sent me from Kadesh Barnea to explore the land. And I brought him back a report according to my convictions, but my brothers who went up with me made the hearts of the people melt with fear. I, however, followed the Lord my God wholeheartedly.

Caleb, Joshua 14:7-8

I want us to look briefly at four Old Testament people who looked fear in the face, fought it, and conquered it: Noah, Abraham, Moses, and Rahab.

God told Noah the tarrying events that would take place in his lifetime. It was enough to scare Superman!

"I will wipe mankind, whom I have created, from the face of the earth," God said (Gen. 6:7). "I am going to put an end to all people, for the earth is filled with violence because of them. I am surely going to destroy both them and the earth" (v. 13).

Imagine Noah's alarm after hearing God's anger and prediction. But Noah trusted and obeyed God. He depended on God's promise of courage as he dreaded upcoming danger. When God told Noah to build a boat, he built it. Noah and his family entered the ark at God's command, closed the door, and then watched the swirling waters rise up around them. They heard the frantic screams of drowning people who beat on the hull of their boat, crying to get inside. They no doubt grieved when they recognized floating corpses of friends and neighbors who had died in the waters. Noah and his family saw their home and familiar habitat swallowed up by floods. They drifted on the sea's surface for forty days and nights, with no land or soul in sight. They persevered when most people would panic. And as a reward for Noah's faithfulness in the face of fear, God gave the world a new future (see Gen. 6-7).

Abram also trusted God. He was already seventy-five years old when God told him to pack up, leave his home and friends, and journey to Canaan—a mysterious, unknown land. Abram depended on God's strength to bring him through the hardships he and his wife, Sarah, encountered on their travels. When Abram grew afraid, God encouraged him: "Do not be afraid, Abram. I am your shield, your very great reward" (Gen. 15:1). Abram, whom God renamed "Abraham," became a first-time father at age 100! One day God severely tested Abraham.

"Take your son...and go to the region of Moriah," God told him. "Sacrifice him there as a burnt offering on one of the mountains I will tell you about (22:2).

Again, Abraham trusted God and obeyed him. The grieving old father took his only son, Isaac, into the mountains, bound the boy, and laid firewood on top of him. Then, just as Abraham raised his knife to kill Isaac, an angel called to him with the welcomed words: "Do not lay a hand on the boy" (v. 12).

God rewarded Abraham for his obedience. "I will surely bless you and make your descendants as numerous as the stars in the sky and as the sand on the seashore...through your offspring all nations on earth will be blessed, because you have obeyed me" (vv. 17-18).

Moses, a Hebrew slave baby in Egypt, escaped a royal death edict when his mother put him in a basket and floated him down the Nile River. His journey brought him into the arms of Pharaoh's daughter, who took him into her home, and raised him like a son. God had great goals for Moses. One day, after Moses became a man, God approached him through a burning bush. The fire burned bright, but it could not consume the bush. The unusual scene, and the sound of God's voice, immediately captured Moses' attention. In great fear, he hid his face (Exod. 3:6).

God commanded Moses to go to Pharaoh and tell him to let the suffering enslaved Israelites leave Egypt. Bewildered by such a task, Moses made multiple excuses, questioned God, and begged the Lord to send someone else to do the job. But, in spite of Moses' reluctance, he finally obeyed, trusting God in faith when he feared certain tragedy. After some extreme "divine persuasion," Pharaoh did let God's people go, and Moses led them on a lengthy wilderness trek toward the Promised Land. Moses' victory over fear, and his faithful obedience, saved a nation.

Rahab, Jericho's infamous prostitute, faced her feelings of panic when Joshua's spies visited her city. At the risk of her life, she defied the king of Jericho by hiding the spies and then helping them escape safely outside the city walls. Because of her obedient trust in God (Josh. 2), her own life, and the lives of her entire family were spared when the Israelites captured the city (Josh. 6).

These true stories are fascinating to read and study. And even though they happened a long time ago, they still speak truth to us today.

These four Old Testament heroes felt great fear, yet they ultimately overcame their fear with obedience to God.

27

More Examples of Old Testament Heroes

Be strong and courageous ... do not be terrified; do not be discouraged, for the Lord your God will be with you wherever you go.

God's words to Joshua in Joshua 1:9

Joshua, Elijah, Esther, and Jonah also faced and fought tremendous fears, and conquered them. We've already read some of Joshua's story in earlier chapters. Now let me fill in the blank spaces of his life. As God's newly appointed leader of the Israelites, Joshua had the huge assignments of following in the footsteps of his great predecessor Moses (itself a daunting task!), and of guiding these oft-sinning people into the Promised Land. Yet Joshua trusted God, following the Lord's specific directions, and was successful in his appointed mission (see the book of Joshua).

Elijah the prophet stood bravely on Mount Carmel before powerful King Ahab and 450 prophets of the pagan god Baal. Jezebel, Ahab's wicked wife, had brutally killed the Lord's prophets. Now face to face with her husband, Elijah challenged the false prophets to a "duel." With great courage, Elijah trusted God, successfully introduced the godless prophets to "the God who answers by fire," and won the contest. Elijah conquered his fear and stood firm in his faith until Jezebel put up an "Elijah Wanted—Dead or Alive" poster. Then great dread overcame Elijah, and he ran away to Horeb.

"Elijah was afraid and ran for his life," Scripture states (1 Kings 19:3). How blessed we are today to see the weaknesses of Biblical characters and not just their strengths! Running away proved Elijah's great weakness. His courage gone, Elijah collapsed in the desert under a broom tree and prayed to die.

That's when God himself challenged his prophet: "Go out and stand on the mountain in the presence of the Lord, for the Lord is about to pass by" (v. 11). In a frightening scenario, Elijah obeyed God. He stood valiantly as a "great and powerful wind tore the mountains apart and shattered the rocks," as an earthquake cracked the mountains, and as fire threatened to consume him. A terrifying chain of events, and Elijah stood right in the middle of the horror.

At last, God came to Elijah in a surprising "gentle whisper," and gave him new instructions. Elijah trusted God's promised courage as he embarked upon new danger, and finally conquered his debilitating fear (see 1 Kings 17–19).

Esther trusted God's promise of hope when she faced possible death. A young Hebrew woman adopted and raised by her cousin, Mordecai, during the exile, Esther became the beautiful bride of Persian King Xerxes. When Mordecai uncovered a political conspiracy to destroy the Jews, he asked Esther to go to the king, beg for his mercy, and save her people. Esther had a right to be afraid. She sent a messenger to tell Mordecai that his idea could cost her her life.

"All the king's officials and the people of the royal provinces know that for any man or woman who approaches the king in the inner court without being summoned the king has but one law: that he be put to death" (Esther 4:11).

Knowing full well what might tragically result, Esther faced her fear. She told Mordecai she would approach the king with his request. And, with her possible punishment fully understood, she bravely added: "And if I perish, I perish" (v. 16).

Queen Esther relied on God for courage when she faced danger. She conquered her fear, spoke with the king, and saved her people. (Read her story in the book of Esther.)

Jonah, like Elijah, caved in to his fear. But, also like Elijah, Jonah recovered, trusted, and obeyed God, and became triumphant over terror. When God told Jonah to "go to the great city of Nineveh and preach against it, because its wickedness has come up before me," Jonah instead boarded a ship headed for Tarshish. He simply ran away instead of obeying God's orders.

But he couldn't hide from God. The Lord sent a violent storm, and Jonah ended up (for three days) inside the belly of a giant God-sent fish. From within the swimming creature, Jonah "identified and examined" his fear of preaching in Nineveh. Then he decided to "face" the danger of Nineveh and preach God's message there. The Lord commanded the fish to vomit Jonah onto dry land, and "Jonah obeyed the word of the Lord and went to Nineveh" (Jonah 3:3). The whole city—120,000 people—repented, fasted, and put on sackcloth after hearing Jonah preach. Even though Jonah grew angry that God spared Nineveh from total destruction (and God had to teach Jonah new lessons), Jonah's reluctant obedience saved Nineveh's people. (Read the story in the book of Jonah.)

Not only does the Old Testament give us accounts of heroes who faced and fought their fear and obeyed God. The New Testament also introduces us to those who triumphed over the fears of tragedy, hardship, death, danger, and loss.

28

Mary, the Amazing Mother of Jesus

I am the Lord's servant. May it be to me as you have said.

Mary's words to Gabriel, when told she was to become the mother of God's Son, Luke 1:38

God also used men and women in New Testament times to accomplish great things for him. Mary proved one remarkable woman who, in spite of fear and uncertainty, trusted and obeyed God.

Mary faced and overcame many frightening situations throughout her lifetime. As a young teenager, Mary had an angelic visitor (we've already seen how such visits from angels terrified other Biblical characters). When Gabriel told Mary she would give birth to the Messiah (Luke 1:26-38), it posed a situation that could have meant Mary's death by stoning. Mary was an unmarried virgin, pledged to Joseph, but now pregnant by the Holy Spirit. The Old Testament—Leviticus 20:10 states the punishment for adultery: "Both the adulterer and the adulteress must be put to death." An engaged woman who became pregnant by another man was proclaimed guilty of adultery. Yet Mary joyfully accepted her possible plight, and gave herself completely to God.

Imagine Mary's grave apprehension as she faced Joseph, her fiancé. Joseph knew for certain that he was not the baby's father, and at first must have logically assumed that Mary had been sexually unfaithful to him. Her pregnancy so flustered Joseph that God sent an angel to dissipate his fears: "Do not be afraid to take Mary home as your wife," the angel told him, "because what is conceived in her is from the Holy Spirit" (Matt. 1:20). Scripture tells us little about Joseph. But in his loving dealings with Mary and her safety, we can assume he, too, faced some giant fears that he had to trust God to overcome.

Mary also had to confront her parents with news of her untimely pregnancy. Did they think that Joseph was the father, or worse? Think about Mary's parents as they struggled to explain their daughter's bulging belly to family members, friends, and neighbors. No doubt, they too feared for their daughter's life as local religious leaders started to question Mary's changing physical condition.

Did Mary's pure and clean reputation take a beating (one that lasted a lifetime?) when she delivered baby Jesus not long after she married Joseph? Did village gossipers gather at the well to count on their fingers, Mary's pregnant months and her married months? One verse of Scripture seems to indicate that even when Jesus was a grown man, Nazareth still regarded Mary as a "mom of ill repute." Preaching in his hometown's synagogue, the people who heard Jesus were amazed at his insightful teachings. Yet with intentional insult and demeaning sarcasm to both Mary and Jesus, they asked: "Where did this man get these things? What's this wisdom that has been given him, that he even does miracles! Isn't this the carpenter? Isn't this Mary's son?" (Mark 6:1-6). In that day and time, had Mary not suffered from societal shame, her neighbors would have politely and respectfully referred to Jesus as "Joseph's son," not "Mary's son."

In spite of her misgivings, Mary clung to God's promises of hope and courage. She faced her pregnancy, and her God-given role, unafraid. God used Mary to give birth to, and rear, Jesus.

After Jesus' birth, Mary and Joseph took their new infant to the temple to be circumcised and consecrated to the Lord. There, Mary met the righteous man Simeon, whose words likely caused her considerable consternation: "This child is destined to cause the falling and rising of many in Israel, and to be a sign that will be spoken against, so that the thoughts of many hearts will be revealed." And then Simeon added, as he probably looked young Mary in the eye: "And a sword will pierce your own soul too" (Luke 2:34-5).

I understood Mary on a deeper level after I saw the film: *The Passion of Christ*. As the mother of a firstborn son, myself, I could only imagine her lifetime of suffering and fear.

Matthew tells us about the couple's sudden terrifying trek to Egypt when Herod sent soldiers to kill all the Hebrew boys two years old and younger. Imagine Mary's fear as she clutched baby Jesus to her breast, and travelled far from home to escape madman Herod's threats (Matt. 2:13-20).

Throughout Jesus' three-year ministry, Mary no doubt heard the reports of her son's narrow escapes from injury and death. With each yearning to understand her remarkable son, Luke states that Mary "treasured all these things in her heart" (Luke 2:51).

Mary also endured her son's arrest and his illegal trials before Caiaphas, the Sanhedrin, and Pilate. She watched Roman soldiers mock and torture Jesus, and then crucify him. She stood beside the cross as Jesus died (John 19:25). Still she trusted God and obeyed.

God rewarded Mary with the motherhood of the Messiah, and with a lasting legacy for all mothers for all time. He blessed Mary with a dedicated, caring son who, in his dying breaths, showed her his everlasting love. "Dear woman, here is your son," Jesus told Mary. And to John the disciple, Jesus said: "Here is your mother." With those words, Jesus entrusted his mother's future care into the hands of John, the beloved disciple (John 19:26-7).

Other men and women, equally as brave as Mary and Joseph, loved, followed, and cared for Jesus during his lifetime. Some risked everything they had to follow him— home, family, livelihood, and life itself. Each faced, fought, and conquered horrifying fears as they witnessed for Christ and gave their lives to his service.

29

The Fearless Witness of Faithful Disciples

And yet, notwithstanding all these continual persecutions and horrible punishments, the Church daily increased, deeply rooted in the doctrine of the apostles and of men apostolical [sic], and watered plentously [sic] with the blood of saints.

From *Fox's Book of Martyrs*

Have you ever wondered what happened to Jesus' followers? Scripture is silent about the fate of most of those who gave up everything to become his disciples. These faithful witnesses faced terrifying situations, overcame their qualms with trust in God, and helped to conquer a world for Christ.

In A.D. 44, James, Jesus' disciple and the son of Zebedee, showed "extraordinary courage and undauntedness" as he met death.

The disciple Philip was scourged, thrown into prison, and then crucified in Phrygia in A.D. 54.

Matthew, the tax collector, was slain with a halberd (a long-handled weapon) in the city of Nadabah in A.D. 60.

James the Less, the possible brother of Jesus, was the disciple who oversaw the Jerusalem churches and wrote the epistle of James. Enraged Jews attacked James, then ninety-four-years old. They beat him, stoned him, and bashed out his brains with a fuller's club – a hammer used to groove and spread iron.

Matthais, the disciple who replaced Judas after Judas betrayed Jesus and hanged himself, was stoned in Jerusalem and beheaded.

Andrew, Peter's brother, was crucified on a cross at Edessa.

Peter was also crucified. Nero ordered Peter's death, but Peter escaped his execution and travelled to the city gates. But, as he stood at the gate, he reported seeing the Lord Christ. Peter courageously returned to the city, faced execution, and was crucified upside-down. An upside-down cross deep in the bowels of Rome's Mamertine Prison reminds us of Peter's cruel imprisonment there and death.

Mark, like Stephen, endured persecution when confronted by an angry mob. They dragged Mark "to pieces" through the streets of Alexandria.

Jude (called Thaddeus), the brother of James, was crucified at Edessa in A.D. 72.

Bartholomew, who courageously took the gospel into India, was severely beaten and crucified.

Thomas (also known as Didymus) was attacked by angry pagan priests who thrust a spear into his body. The Romans, at that time, worshipped many pagan "gods" and built elaborate temples as a place to worship them. Many of these temples are still standing throughout the old Roman Empire.

Luke was hanged on an olive tree by the idolatrous priests of Greece.

Simon was crucified in A.D. 74.

John, the "beloved disciple" (who founded the churches of Smyrna, Pergamos, Sardis, Philadelphia, Laodicea, and

Thyatira, and who took care of Mary after Jesus' death), was ordered to Rome to be "cast into a cauldron of boiling oil." He escaped without injury, however. Domitian later banished him to the isle of Patmos, where he experienced terrifying visions and wrote the book of Revelation. John was the only apostle who escaped a violent death.

These men faced horrifying situations. They experienced fear time and again through physical pain, cruel torture, and the threat of an agonizing death. Yet they stood up to fear, and they walked courageously to their deaths in Christ's name.

30

Dedicated, Dauntless and Joyful Martyrs

For the Spirit God gave us does not make us timid, but gives us power, love, and self-discipline.

Paul's words to Timothy, 2 Timothy 1:7

Paul had entered his final years of active ministry when, from prison, he wrote to encourage his protégé Timothy. Paul urges his "true son in the faith" to put away timidity, and to preach boldly Christ's message.

"Fight the good fight," he tells the young pastor (1 Tim. 1:18). Paul also warns Timothy about future horrors that might happen because of Timothy's preaching. "Persevere," Paul tells him. And don't "let anyone look down on you because you are young" (4:12, 16). Paul invites Timothy to join him "in suffering for the gospel, by the power of God," and to "be strong." Paul assures him that Christ Jesus "has destroyed death" (2 Tim. 1:8, 10). As Paul himself faces upcoming death, he urges Timothy to "preach the Word," and to "keep your head in all situations, endure hardship, do the work of an evangelist" (4:2, 5).

Paul knew about fear, danger, suffering, and hardship. Throughout the years of his ministry, Paul endured imprisonment, severe floggings, beatings, stonings, and terrifying shipwrecks. He often lacked food, water, clothes, heat, and sleep, yet he continued to preach and labor for Christ. Paul looked to the Lord to help him triumph over his weaknesses and fears. He writes: "That is why, for Christ's sake, I delight in weaknesses, in insults, in hardships, in persecutions, in difficulties. For when I am weak, then I am strong" (2 Cor. 12:10).

Paul understood that Timothy would probably face painful persecution because of his Christian witness. Not long after Paul wrote his letter to Timothy [the book of 2 Timothy], under Nero's Christian persecutions, Paul himself was beheaded.

Timothy took Paul's advice. He preached, he became the bishop of Ephesus, and he led the church courageously until A.D. 97. A strong Christian leader, during the second persecution (under Domitian), Timothy reprimanded the city's godless people as they gathered to celebrate a pagan feast. An angry crowd pounced on him and beat him with clubs. Timothy suffered agonizing pain for two days and then he died.[1]

Other believers throughout the early church suffered intense pain and miserable deaths. But they faced them in Christ's name, unafraid, and often with joy and thanksgiving.

During the Fifth Christian Persecution, a twenty-two-year-old wife and new mother, Perpetua, along with her maid, Felicitas, were condemned to death for following

---

1   http://www.reformed.org/books/fox/DOCS/fox102.html. July 26, 2004. From *Fox's Book of Martyrs*.

Christ. Perpetua's father begged her to turn away from her faith, to denounce Christ, to offer the required pagan sacrifices, and to save herself. But she refused. She would not allow the fear of suffering and death to turn her away from Christ.

During her imprisonment, Perpetua kept a diary. She wrote: "A few days later we were lodged in the prison; and I was terrified, as I had never before been in such a dark hole. What a difficult time it was! With the crowd the heat was stifling; then there was the extortion of the soldiers; and to crown all I was tortured with worry for my baby there. Then Tertius and Pomponius, those blessed deacons who tried to take care of us, bribed the soldiers to allow us to go to a better part of the prison to refresh ourselves for a few hours. Everyone then left that dungeon and shifted for himself. I nursed my baby, who was faint from hunger. In my anxiety I spoke to my mother about the child, I tried to comfort my brother, and I gave the child in their charge. I was in pain because I saw them suffering out of pity for me. These were the trials I had to endure for many days. Then I got permission for my baby to stay with me in prison."

Shortly before her death, Perpetua's father again came to see her.

"Daughter," he said, "have pity on my grey head—have pity on me your father, if I deserve to be called your father, if I have favoured you above all your brothers, if I have raised you to reach this prime of your life. Do not abandon me to be the reproach of men. Think of your brothers, think of your mother and your aunt, think of your child, who will not be able to live once you are gone. Give up your pride! You will destroy all of us! None of us will ever be able to speak freely again if anything happens to you."

Perpetua writes: "This was the way my father spoke out of love for me, kissing my hands and throwing himself down before me. With tears in his eyes, he no longer addressed me as his daughter but as a woman. I was sorry for my father's sake, because he alone of all my kin would be unhappy to see me suffer."

Felicitas, Perpertua's maid, was expecting a child when she was arrested. Eight months pregnant, the law forbade expectant mothers to be executed. Two days before her scheduled public execution, Felicitas went into labor, suffered excruciating birth pains, and delivered a baby girl.

During the painful birth, one of the prison guards taunted Felicitas: "You suffer so much now—what will you do when you are tossed to the beasts? Little did you think of them when you refused to sacrifice [to recant her faith]."

Felicitas answered the cruel guard with courage: "What I am suffering now," she replied, "I suffer by myself. But then another will be inside me who will suffer for me, just as I shall be suffering for him."

When the time for execution came, Perpetua, Felicitas, and the other sentenced Christians "marched from the prison to the amphitheatre joyfully as thought they were going to heaven, with calm faces, trembling, if at all, with joy rather than fear. Perpetua went along with shining countenance and calm step, as the beloved of God, as a wife of Christ, putting down everyone's stare by her own intense gaze. With them also was Felicitas, glad that she had safely given birth so that now she could fight the beasts, going from one blood bath to another, from the midwife to the gladiator, ready to wash after childbirth in a second baptism."

The two women "were stripped naked, placed in nets and thus brought out into the arena. Even the crowd was horrified when they saw that one was a delicate young girl and the other was a woman fresh from childbirth with the milk still dripping from her breasts."[2]

Perpetua and Felicitas were thrown to a mad bull. The bull first attacked Perpetua, and stunned her. Then the bull gored Felicitas. Both women survived the savage attack, and as they lay broken and bleeding, an executioner stabbed them, killing both with his sword.

Those Christians who died with them that day were Revocatus and Satur (destroyed by wild beasts), Saturninus (beheaded), and Secundulus (who died in prison). Each faced death with courage, ready and willing to die for their faith in Christ.[3]

You and I may never have to face suffering and death like Perpetua, Felicitas, and others for their public faith in Christ. But we can learn how to live with faith and courage, dependent on God in our lives and deaths and sufferings, through their courageous examples.

Don't allow fear to deter you from reaching your potential for life and ministry. You can find freedom from it. You can conquer it, with God's help.

---

2   The quotes used in the account of Perpetua and Felicitas are from an online source: *The Acts of the Christian Martyrs*, texts and translation by Herbert Musurillo, Oxford University Press, 1972, found at: http://www.pbs.org/wgbh/pages/frontline/ shows/religion/maps/primary/perpetua. Html, accessed July 26, 2004.

3   [http://www.reformed.org/books/fox/DOCS/fox102.html. July 26, 2004. From *Fox's Book of Martyrs*.

Bible Study Section For Personal Reflection and Study

Section 1: What Women Fear

Ch. 1: The Fear of Life's Unexpected Storms

1. Scripture mentions many types of storms that biblical characters faced. Read Matthew 14:1-12; 15:21-28; and 19:16-30, and list the "storm" each person faced. Now, compare their experiences with your own. Can you identify with the troubles that worried them? If so, how?

2. Have you ever allowed your own fear of losing something—possessions, relationship, or reputation—to come between you and God? Briefly explain the situation and how your fellowship with God ended up being restored.

   Prayer to pray: *Father, it seems that to be human is to be afraid. I look around me and see so many things to fear. Storms seem to surround me. Help me to trust you, Lord, in the midst of all current and future storms. Teach me how to depend on you, and to meet fear with faith's courage. Assure me, Father, that you do indeed keep your deep-root promises as written in your Word. In Jesus' name I pray, amen.*

Ch. 2: The Fear of Death

1. Read Romans 8:38-39. Note all the things that Scripture says cannot separate you from God's love. From this list, what do you personally fear might separate you from God, and why?

2. List three things that frighten you most about death.

3. List three questions you'd like to ask God about death.

4. Pray about the fears you just listed. Ask God to guide you into understanding.

    Prayer to pray: *Lord, death seems so mysterious to me. I fear what will happen when I close my eyes and depart this life. Help me to know that, when that happens, you will be with me. Calm my fear of death's storm, Lord, just like you calmed the disciples' fears during the storm on Lake Galilee. Teach me to depend solely on faith in you when I think about and confront my death. In Jesus' name, amen.*

Ch. 3: The Fear of Physical Harm, Violence, Hate Crime, and Evil

1. Read Hebrews 13:6. Write it on an index card and tape it to your bathroom mirror. Read it each morning as you dress for the day.

2. Name three concerns or problems you have worried about in the past that never happened. Then, write down why you worried about those things? Answer: How could you have better used that "worry time"?

<u>Prayer to pray</u>: *Lord, keep me and my loved ones safe from those people who want to hurt us. Give me the courage not to be afraid that I might encounter crime. Please don't allow the Evil One to prey on my fears of violence. Protect me and those I love. Help me to be cautious. But keep me from being afraid. In Jesus' name, amen.*

Ch. 4: The Fear of Losing Loved Ones

1. Read Psalm 27:10. What is David's assurance to you about God's presence?

2. How can you personally gain strength from David's words when you face crises and feel afraid and alone?

3. Think of a time or two when you felt afraid and turned to Scripture for courage. Explain the situation(s) and the Scripture verse(s) that helped you most.

<u>Prayer to Pray</u>: *Lord, I take your words from Scripture to my heart. Help me to listen to you when you tell me not to be*

*afraid. Help me to know for sure that you are always with
me—that I can be full of faith. In Jesus' name, amen.*

Ch. 5: Fear, The Number-One Emotional Issue for Women

1. Ask God to give you clear recall of your most
   significant past fears.

2. Also ask his help in identifying your most significant present fears.

3. Write down your present fears—all those things
   you are presently dealing with. By each fear, explain
   why you are afraid of each particular thing.

   <u>Prayer to Pray</u>: *Lord, fear seems to be a way of life
   for women today. We have so many responsibilities, so
   many people who depend on us, so many things we want to
   accomplish. In the midst of our many responsibilities—
   family, careers, aging parents, children—we often must face
   heartbreak, confusion, conflict, physical and emotional pain,
   spiritual emptiness, financial pressures, wayward children,
   mental health problems, and other unexpected storms. We
   grow tired, Lord. There is too much to do, and not nearly
   enough time or energy to get it all done. The stress of life
   makes us afraid. We fear we cannot keep up with all that
   life requires. You promise us your presence, Lord. Please be
   near, especially during those times we face pain and grief and
   loss. I will depend on you, Lord, to comfort me and guide me
   throughout the days of my life. In Jesus' name I pray, amen.*

Section 2: Examine Your Fears—Healthy Fear, God's Gift that Arms You

Ch. 6: Wise Women Fear God

1. Read John 3:16. What is God's promise and how does it relate personally to you?

2. Read John 1:5. Name a time in your life when you "lacked wisdom." How did you handle it?

3. Write in your own words what it means to "fear" God. In what ways do you personally "fear" God?

4. What reward does God give you when you "fear" him? (See Ps. 19:9-11).

   Prayer to Pray: *Lord, your Word tells me to fear you. Help me to understand exactly what "fearing you" means. I hold you in awe, Lord, in great respect, and with admiring love. You are my Holy Creator, Father. I am just a weak creature. Show me how to depend on you. Teach me how to read and understand your Word. Lead me to want to keep your commandments, and to live a life that will honor you. In Jesus' name, amen.*

Ch. 7: Healthy Fear Demands Your Undivided Attention

1. Read Daniel 8:16-26; 9:20-27; 10:9-19; and Luke 1:11-20. Reflect on what these passages mean.

2. Think about the events that caused you most fear. How did they capture your attention? What was your immediate reaction caused by fear? What did you learn from them?

Prayer to Pray: *Lord, I can identify with the reactions of Daniel, Zechariah, and the shepherds when they first saw an angel. I too have been face-to-face with terror. You have given me a wonderful gift, Lord—the gift of healthy fear. It has protected me in my terror. You have created within me an automatic survival response that aims to protect my life from predators. I praise you because I am fearfully and wonderfully made. Your works are wonderful, Lord. Thank you! In Jesus' name, I pray, amen.*

Ch. 8: How Your Body Responds to Healthy Fear

1. Read Scripture verses: John 18:6, 10 and Luke 24:5.

2. Take a moment to imagine these scenes from Scripture taking place. What do you see happening? Describe each person's physical expression of fear. Have you ever felt your own body and mind react in these or similar ways? If so, please describe. What situations did you face at the time?

Prayer to Pray: *Lord, I thank you that my body serves me so well. It seeks to protect me when I face danger. I know that when I need extra strength and keener decision-making abilities, you have created within me those qualities. I love you, Lord. You tell me you were with me before I was ever born. No matter where I go, Lord, you are there. You tell me that you have ordained for me all the days of my life. You have a special purpose for my life. I pray I can be a good disciple. In Jesus' name, amen.*

Ch. 9: How A.R.M.S. Fear Can Save Your Life

1. Read Psalm 139. List all the ways this passage comforts you.

2. Name some of those times when A.R.M.S. healthy fear helped you address and deal with some common everyday situations.

   <u>Prayer to Pray</u>: *Lord, your Word tells me that you keep me from all harm. You watch over my life—my coming and my going both now and forevermore. With this assurance, Lord, I will not fear. You also tell me that you command your angels concerning me. They guard me in all my ways. They lift me up in their hands, so I will not strike my foot against a stone. How can I fear, Lord, in the knowledge of your Word? I will look to you, Lord, at all times, and especially in times of danger. In Jesus' name I pray, amen.*

Ch. 10: You Are Created to Survive

1. Write down those things that presently bring you fear. Tell why they cause you fear.

2. Examine those fears you listed. Circle each fear you regard as a healthy, life-saving fear.

<u>Prayer to Pray</u>: *Lord, thank you for all your blessings to me, and to those I love. I love you, Lord. My desire in life is to serve you, to do your kingdom work. Strengthen me, guide me, enable me to examine those fears that keep me from accomplishing what you've called me to do. Show me how to use healthy fear to preserve my life. I pray, Lord, that women everywhere will discover their remarkable gifts of healthy fear. I pray they will give you the glory and the credit for this magnificent gift. In Jesus' name I pray, amen.*

SECTION 3: Unhealthy Fear—Satan's Tool That Harms You

Ch. 11: Unhealthy Fear Is Satan's Instrument

Choose one of these Scripture passages—Genesis 1, Genesis 3, or 1 John 5—read it, and answer the following questions.

a. Genesis 1: How do you think your life would have been different before sin entered the human race? If you'd like, on a sheet of paper roughly sketch the way you think the first garden looked after God created it. Draw a figure of yourself in the garden.

b. Genesis 3: Reflect on how your life has been changed by sin and unhealthy fear.

c. 1 John 5: Explain in one paragraph what John tells his readers. What does John mean when he writes: "We know that we are children of God, and that the whole world is under the control of the evil one" (v. 19)? In what ways has the "evil one" influenced, changed, or interfered in your life? Or in the lives of your loved ones?

Prayer to Pray: *Lord I can rest in the fact that you care for me. Even though the whole world seems to be under the control of the Evil One, I need not be afraid. You are always with me, protecting, guiding, and helping me. Lord, I want to cry when I see how sin has ruined the beauty of the world you created. I pray that you will use me to spread the good news of the gospel and proclaim that you give Living Water to those who are afraid and thirsty. In Jesus' name I pray, amen.*

Ch. 12: Women And Panic Attacks

1. Review the definition of a panic disorder from this chapter. Have you ever experienced a panic attack? If so, how did it affect you—physically, emotionally, mentally?

2. What is a believer's primary purpose in life, and how can a panic disorder distort or change it?

3. What is your personal primary purpose in life? Have you ever allowed fear (in the form of a panic disorder) to render you ineffective in pursuing your purpose?

   <u>Prayer to Pray</u>: *Thank you, Lord, that I don't have to fear those things that aren't real. Keep me from my imaginary fears—those unhealthy fears that start with thoughts and end up in panic disorders. Show me how to defeat the Evil One, who tries to trip up believers and frighten us and keep us from working in your kingdom. In Jesus' name I pray, amen.*

Ch. 13: Women and Post-Traumatic Stress Disorder

1. Whether you're experiencing post-traumatic stress disorder or the stressful issues of everyday life, Psalm 139 is a wonderful Scripture passage to cling to. Read the psalm slowly and aloud.

2. Write on an index card those verses from Psalm 139 that bring you hope and comfort. Place the card

in the front of your Bible, and read it at least once a day for a week. Let God's Word assure you that you are precious to him, that he knows your mind and experiences, and that he is always near you.

<u>Prayer to Pray</u>: *Lord, I pray that you will bring me your reassurance as I face each day with its traumas and indecision and stress. Keep me safe from those experiences that could hurt me. Heal my unpleasant memories that refuse to be quieted. Please let me rest my mind in you and in your Word. Bring me peace. Father, I also want to pray for women today who suffer painful trials in their lives. How we each long for healing when we suffer from nightmares and misery related to traumatic events. I pray for the protection of women in this world. I pray for those women living in countries that hurt them, torture them, and claim their freedoms. Show yourself to those hurting women, Lord. Be near to them, and bring them to trust and have faith in you. In Jesus' name I pray. Amen.*

Ch. 14: Women and Anxiety

1. Read the following Scripture verses to see what the Bible says about anxiety: Psalm 55:22; Isaiah 41:13; Matthew 6:25. Make notes as you read, and refer to them any time you feel worried or anxious.

2. On an index card, write down the wisdom of 1 Peter 5:7 ("Cast all your anxiety on him because he cares for you"), and attach it to your refrigerator or bathroom mirror. As you reread its message day by day, jot down

(underneath the verse) some of the anxieties you are feeling. Take time to pray about each one, petitioning God—with thanksgiving—to give you his calm peace.

Prayer to Pray: *Lord, I pray for those women who feel anxious or worried. Help them to understand that their lives are too precious to you, and to those who love them, to be filled with fret and unease. Calm their minds, Lord. Show them that you offer abundant, joyful life—life that need not be discouraged or distressed by severe anxiety disorders or even everyday feelings of helplessness and worry. Keep me also, Father, from worry and anxious thoughts. Show me how to pray, petition, and be thankful. Teach me how to use your Word to see me calmly through each troubling day. I want the peace of God that transcends all understanding. Please, Lord, guard my heart and my mind in Christ Jesus. In Jesus' name I pray, amen.*

Ch. 15: Women and Phobias

1. Memorize Romans 8:38-39. Whenever you feel any type of fear, recite aloud these two verses.

2. Make a list of your unhealthy fears, and explain why each one is unhealthy.

3. Review your list, examine each unhealthy fear, and determine if this fear might be a phobia. (The guide for making that determination is below):[1]

   a. Are you genuinely "afraid" of things like high places, dogs, snakes, flying, etc? Or

---

1 Note: If you answered "yes" to these three questions (following), then you may be dealing with a phobia. You may want to seek out a Christian counselor to help you with these fears.

could you possibly be using the word "afraid" when you really mean you have a "healthy respect for" high places, dogs, snakes, flying, etc.?

b. Does this "fear" of some thing, animal or person, interrupt your life, work, relationships, and/or worship in such a significant way that you are unable to function in everyday life?

c. Does your "fear" of social situations, such as meeting new people or speaking in public, keep you from going to work, church, the grocery store, or to the homes of friends?

Prayer to Pray: *Father, I understand the difference between my healthy fears and my unhealthy fears. I have examined my fears and labeled each one "healthy" or "unhealthy." Now, Lord, with your help and guidance, I am ready to face my fears. Please show me your promises that I can keep in my heart when I face unhealthy fear. Direct me to your examples so that I may know how to respond to unhealthy fear. As I continue to study your Word, Lord, I am encouraged I can face and overcome my unhealthy fears. Thank you, Lord. I know that the deeper my roots dig into your Word, the stronger my foundation of faith becomes. In Jesus' name I pray, amen.*

SECTION 4: Face Your Fears

Ch. 16: Face Fear with God's Promises

1. Read Mark 11:12-25. Describe the story, what happened, and, in your opinion, why Jesus said, "Have faith in God" (v. 22).

2. Have you ever faced and conquered your fear of tragedy with faith in Christ? Is so, reflect on it.

3. Read Romans 3:9-31. What did Paul say about faith and righteousness? How do Paul's words help you in your own life?

   Prayer to Pray: *Lord, please give me the faith of the bleeding woman who touched the hem of your robe and was healed. I pray for deepening faith, Lord, when I face tragedy. I pray for the sound of your healing words when I face painful trials. Speak to me the words you spoke to her, Father, when you said, "Your faith has healed you. Go in peace and be freed from your suffering." In Jesus' name I pray, amen.*

Ch. 17: God Promises You Strength When You Fear Hardship

1. Read John 4:24; 14:26; Acts 2:38; Romans 8:26; 1 Corinthians 6:19; 12:13; and Ephesians 2:18. Ponder these questions:

   a. What comforts do these verses about the Holy Spirit bring you?

b. Where do you most need comfort right now and why?

c. Robertson McQuilkin's book, *A Promise Kept*, is one of the most beautiful and encouraging books I've read. If possible, buy a copy or check one out of your local library and read this week.

Prayer to Pray: *Lord, teach me about strong faith through the lives of people like Dr. McQuilkin. Let me depend on your Word when I fear hardships and need strength. You promise me strength when I need it. Let me take your words to heart, believe them without doubt, and practice them in my daily life. In Jesus' name I pray, amen.*

Ch. 18: God Promises You Hope When You Fear the Process of Dying

1. Read the following Scripture passages. In a short summary paragraph, list what each one promises you, and what each promise means to you personally: Isaiah 57:2, Romans 6:1-23; and 1 Corinthians 15:1-58.

2. Name at least three things Scripture says about death and dying in Ecclesiastes 3:1-2; 7:2; and Hebrews 9:27.

3. Note the ways these passages comfort you and bring you hope. Memorize a verse that is particularly meaningful and helpful to you.

Prayer to Pray: *Lord, because you love me and gave yourself for me, I thank you. You have promised me, your daughter, eternal life when I die. I believe your Word, Lord. I will not fear death. Help me also to be unafraid of the actual process of dying. Whether it be sudden and painless, or long and painful, help me keep my eyes focused on the end result of my dying—my coming home to you. Thank you for your Word that promises me I won't go through the journey of dying by myself, but that you will be with me. In Jesus' name I pray, amen.*

Ch. 19: God Promises You Courage When You Fear Danger

1. To arm you in times when you face danger, memorize at least one of the following Bible verses:

    a. Psalm 91:1-2: "He who dwells in the shelter of the Most High will rest in the shadow of the Almighty. I will say of the Lord, 'He is my refuge and my fortress, my God, in whom I trust.'"

    b. Psalm 121:7-8: "The Lord will keep you from all harm—he will watch over your life; the Lord will watch over your coming and going both now and forevermore."

    c. Isaiah 43:1-5: "But now, this is what the Lord says—he who created you, O Jacob, he who formed you, O Israel: 'Fear not, for I have redeemed you; I have summoned you by name; you are mine. When you pass through the waters, I will be with you; and when you pass through the rivers, they will not sweep over you. When you walk through the fire you will not be burned; the flames will not set you ablaze...Do not be afraid, for I am with you."

2. The book of Esther shows a young woman's courage in the midst of terrible, frightening tragedy. Read her remarkable story in Esther 3–8. As you read, jot down the qualities you find in Esther's life. What attributes of Esther do you find (or would like to have) in your own life?

   Prayer to Pray: *Lord, I am inclined to pray for courage—courage that would help me stand strong against any fear I encounter. But, Lord, I don't pray for courage. Instead I pray for faith—a stronger, surer faith in you and in your Word. For I know that when I face danger, if I stand on faith, you will give me the courage I need to deal with my fears. In Jesus' name I pray, amen.*

Ch. 20: God Promises You Comfort When You Fear Loss

1. Visit your local library (or use the Internet) and study the life of Martin Luther. You will be amazed at this courageous man's life.

2. As you read, ask God to incorporate into your own life those attributes shown by Martin Luther.

   Prayer to Pray: *Lord, I stand with faith on the promises you make to me in your precious Word. They are my hope.*

They are my rock-solid foundation. Thank you for them. With you, Father, I can face those fears that cause me to tremble. I can deal with those fears that disrupt and distress my life. Keep me in the center of your will for my life. You have gifted me to do my unique job here on earth. I pray I can fulfill my role and finish my job.

Lord, when I experience unhealthy fear, I pray you will teach me to face it and conquer it. I pray you will prevent Satan from using his tools of unhealthy fear to deter my work, drain my energy, and devour my times. Help me, Lord, to trust your promises.

Lord, I also want to pray for all those women around the world who cope with unhealthy fears. Put your arms around those who fear and face tragedy, hardship, dying, danger, and loss. Teach them your promises, so that they too may stand firm in faith and depend on prayer. In Jesus' name I pray, amen.

Section 5: Conquer Your Fears with Christ's Example

Ch. 21: Conquer Fear of Evil with Christ's Words

1. Look up and read the following references: Isaiah 14:12; Ezekiel 28:11-16; Matthew 6:13; 12:24, 27; Luke 11:15; 1 Corinthians 7:5. What does Scripture tell you about Satan?

2. How can these words from God give you courage and hope?

3. Name three reasons why you need not fear the Evil One.

4. How can you use Jesus' examples in Matthew 4:1-11 to resist Satan?

    Prayer to Pray: *Lord, you will protect me from the Evil One. Satan cannot hurt me. You, my Father, are more powerful than Satan. I am your daughter, and I need not fear evil. I pray that I might follow your example, Lord. When I am tempted to fear, teach me to confront Satan's attacks with Scripture. In Jesus' name I pray, amen.*

Ch. 22: Conquer Fear of Hate with Christ's Love

1. Read the following passages and write down the advice Scripture gives regarding love: Romans 12:10; 1 Corinthians 16:14; and Galatians 5:13.

2. In light of your own fears of hate, what do these verses say to you?

3. List the attributes of love as described in 1 Corinthians 13. Then circle the descriptions of love that you most wish to cultivate in your own life and relationships.

4. If put into practice, think about how these characteristics relieve your fears of hatred? How can they help change the fearful society in which you live?

Prayer to Pray: *Lord, when I face hate and feel its fear, help me to overcome and conquer hate with your love. Thank you for your example. In Jesus' name I pray, amen.*

Ch. 23: Conquer Fear of Cruelty with Christ's Forgiveness

1. Read the following passages: Matthew 6:14; 18:21; Ephesians 4:32; Philippians 3:13; and Colossians 3:13. Then choose the one verse you most relate to and write down why.

2. If you have access to a newspaper, find at least five articles that deal with human cruelty toward a woman. Examine each one. Write down the ways that particular cruelty hurt the woman involved. Pray a prayer for her, using her name and situation.

Prayer to Pray: *Lord, you have forgiven me of my many sins and wrongdoings. Help me to forgive others who sin against me. I pray I can show the faith of Beth Nimmo and Darrell Scott when they forgave Rachel's killers. I pray that when I encounter cruelty—as I surely will—I will follow your example and forgive. In Jesus' name I pray, amen.*

Ch. 24: Conquer Fear of Fear with Christ's Courage

1. Read the story of Joshua and Caleb found in Numbers 13:1-14; 38; Deuteronomy 1:36; and Joshua 14:6; 15;19. In most situations (where fear might influence a decision), do you most readily identify with Joshua and Caleb (and exhibit bravery) or the ten spies (who allowed the fear of fear to make their decision)? Explain.

2. What attributes shown by Joshua and Caleb do you hope to more deeply develop in your own life, and why?

3. What can these two men teach you about taking a risk and trusting God with your fears?

Prayer to pray: *Lord, I pray for the courage shown by Joshua and Caleb. In spite of their fears, they trusted you. They believed your Word and your promises. You gave each man the courage to confront and conquer his fears. Lord, whenever I am afraid, whenever fear makes me want to turn away or procrastinate making a decision, help me to face my fears with your courageous examples, and conquer them. In Jesus' name I pray, amen.*

Ch. 25: Conquer Fear of Suffering with Christ's Acceptance

1. What especially "spoke" to you in this chapter? Why?

2. What have you learned so far about fear—healthy fear and unhealthy fear? Ponder your answers.

Prayer to Pray: *Lord, let me face evil with your Word. Let me fight hate with you love. Let me confront cruelty with your forgiveness. Let me tackle fear with your courage. And when I face dying, allow me to learn how to leave this physical life with dignity, grace, anticipation, and acceptance. Lord, thank you that you have given me your promises to depend on, and your examples to follow, whenever I encounter fear. Help me to be quick to identify each fear, and wise enough to examine it and name it. Please give me the courage and strength to take each unhealthy fear to you in prayer, and to leave it with you. Thank you for your perfect peace—a peace beyond all human understanding. In Jesus' name, amen.*

SECTION 6: Testimonies of Fears Conquered

Ch. 26: Old Testament Heroes We Should All Know About

1. Choose one of today's Old Testament heroes, read what Scripture says about him or her, and answer the questions below:

   a. Noah: read Genesis 6-7

   b. Abraham: read Genesis 15-22

   c. Moses: read Exodus 1-14

   d. Rahab: read Joshua 2

2. In your reading, what did you discover about the courage of the biblical character you chose?

3. Have you ever shown bravery in the face of fear like this biblical character? If so, take a few minutes to remember the event.

4. In what ways would you like to resemble this particular Old Testament character and why?

Prayer to Pray: *Father, when I confront future fear, and must make the decision to obey you or run away, please help me to take the challenge, confront my fear, and trust and obey you. Thank you for showing me how men and women of long ago fought fearfulness and won a victory for all of us. In Jesus' name, amen.*

Ch. 27: More Examples of Old Testament Heroes

1. Choose one of the Old Testament heroes from this chapter, and read the suggested Scripture that tells that hero's story:

    a. Joshua: the book of Joshua

    b. Elijah: 1 Kings 17-19

    c. Esther: the book of Esther

    d. Jonah: the book of Jonah

2. What strengths did your chosen Old Testament hero have that you most want in your own life? Explain why.

3. In what ways do you identify with the hero you chose to study?

4. Why is it important for you, and other believers, to examine the lives and fears of biblical characters?

<u>Prayer to Pray</u>: *Father, I pray that you might make me as courageous as Joshua and Esther when they trusted God and never once doubted. Make me less like Elijah and Jonah when they gave in to fear and tried to escape your purpose. Help me to follow you, accomplish the goals you have set for me, and to never question your commands. In Jesus' name, amen.*

Ch. 28: Mary, the Amazing Mother of Jesus

1. Read the following Scripture verses: Luke 1:26-38; Leviticus 20:10; Matthew 1:20; 2:13-20; Luke 2:51; and John 19:25-27. Now ponder these questions:

    a. In what ways do you most respect Mary, the mother of Jesus?

    b. How does Mary's reaction to justified fear give you courage and strength?

2. Search through Matthew, Mark, Luke, and John, and list other women who showed unusual courage in times of great fear. What characteristics of their lives do you most want to incorporate into your own life, and why?

    Prayer to Pray: *Father, I too want to be a courageous woman. Like Mary, help me to act on your commands without hesitation and in spite of my fears. Show me how to trust you so completely that I set aside my reservations and follow you, even if it means danger or injury or death. Thank you, Lord, for Mary, for her compassion and care for Jesus, our Savior. In Jesus' name I pray, amen.*

Ch. 29: The Fearless Witness of Faithful Disciples

1. Read Matthew 4:21-22. Who was John's brother? How did the two brothers respond to Jesus' call? Did they regard the call from Jesus with fear? Why or why not?

2. Read Mark 9:1-13. Describe the events at the transfiguration where John was present. How might this event have prepared him for the future?

3. Read Acts 4:1-3 and Galatians 2:9. In what ways did John help establish the church? During these times of persecution, how do you think John responded to the ever-present fear that surrounded him?

4. Read Revelation 1:21-3. For what purpose did John write Revelation? Now read Revelation 1:9-17. How did John react to the terrifying visions? (v. 17) How did the Lord comfort him? (vv. 17-18)

Prayer to Pray: *Father, make me like your servants— loyal, diligent, and unafraid to follow you. I thank you, Lord, for all the saints I read about today—for their leadership, their selfless lives, their remarkable testimonies, and for their boldness as they suffered beating, stoning, stabbing, crucifixion, and, like John, lonely isolation in his final days. In Jesus' name I pray, amen.*

Chapter 30: "Dedicated, Dauntless, and Joyful Martyrs"

1. List the people in this chapter you read about. Describe two personal attributes, shown by each person, that you most admire.

2. How did each person follow Christ's example?

<u>Prayer to Pray</u>: *Father, please forgive me for all the ways I have allowed my fears and worries to overwhelm me and keep me from my God-given purpose in life. I have failed you, Father, in so many ways. And I am sorry, Lord. I pray for your strength in the future as I strive to follow the inspiring examples of those Old and New Testament heroes of the faith, as well as those martyrs throughout church history—even to this day—who showed such courage in the face of chilling fear. Give me new purpose, Father, and a new dedication and commitment to labor in your work, to produce a fruitful witness for Christ, and to leave a lasting example and legacy for future believers to follow. Help me to realize that I too, like Paul, can "do everything through him who gives me strength." I pray all these things in Jesus' name, amen.*

Bible Studies for Group Discussion

Section 1: What Women Fear

Ask your group of women to read Chapters 1-5. Meet together, and participate in the Group Bible Study:

1. Briefly share a highlight from Chapters 1-5 that particularly "spoke" to you, and explain why.

2. Think for a moment about your closest friends. Then make a mental list of each friend's most significant fear or worry. Without using names or specific circumstances, go around the group mentioning the various fears you're aware of. Then briefly discuss some of the things that struck you about this exercise.

3. Read aloud Colossians 3:12-17. Then, as a group, name the ways listed in this passage that God calls us, as Christian women, to live.

4. Discuss: By following these scriptural mandates, how can we avoid becoming victims to worry and fear?

5. Discuss your definition of "peace." Then address these questions: What is the "peace of Christ"? How is it different from the "peace" the world offers?

Group Prayer to Pray: *Lord, we don't want fear to be the number-one emotional issue in our lives. Please take away our fears, and let us trust you. Help us to know that you hold the future, and we don't need to be afraid. You know what tomorrow will bring, even if we don't. Show us how to serve you, Lord. Create in us the discipline to devote ourselves to prayer, and to be watchful and thankful. In Jesus' name we pray, amen.*

SECTION 2: Examine Your Fears: Healthy Fear – God's Gift That Arms You

Ask your group of women to read Chapters 6-10. Meet together, and participate in the Group Bible Study:

1. Briefly share a highlight in chapters 6-10 that particularly spoke to you.

2. Taking turns, read 1 Samuel 17:1-58, and, as a group, answer the following questions:

   a. How did the Israelites react to Goliath when the giant challenged them to battle? Compare their response to David's.

   b. Do you think David had a healthy or unhealthy fear of Goliath? Explain.

   c. What evidences do you see that David's fear of God exceeded his fear of Goliath?

   d. What impresses you most about David in this story?

   e. Discuss a time when you reacted poorly to healthy fear that presented itself in an everyday or traumatic situation. What faith lesson, of any, did you learn from the experience?

f. Now share about a frightening time in which, like David, you showed unusual courage (faith) when no one else rose to the challenge. What spiritual lessons did you learn?

Group Prayer to Pray: *Lord, we so admire David when he stood up and fought against Goliath when everyone else turned and fled. Thank you for showing us this example of faith-based courage in the face of extreme danger. Help us, Father, to be like David. Help us to always know that we can do everything through you, the one who gives us strength. In Jesus' name, amen.*

SECTION 3: Examine Your Fears: Unhealthy Fear – Satan's Tool That Harms You

Ask your group of women to read Chapters 11-15. Meet together, and participate in the Group Bible Study:

1. In Chapters 11-15, each woman in the group has learned about various types of unhealthy fear: panic attacks, post-traumatic stress disorder, anxiety, and phobias. In this group study, concentrate specifically on phobias: specific or special phobias, social situation phobias, and agoraphobia. Taking turns, read aloud the next three paragraphs:

    a. Specific or special phobias are fears of things like snakes (*ophidiophobia*), birds (*ornithophobia*), cats (*ailurophobia*), spiders (*arachnophobia*), tombstones (*placophobia*), dirt (*rupophobia*), etc. They can also include fears of heights (*acrophobia*), empty spaces (*kenophobia*), lakes (*limnophobia*), etc.

    b. Social phobias are fears relating to social situations, such as speaking in public (*glossophobia*), meeting strangers (*xenophobia*), being stared at (*ophthalmophobia*), etc.

    c. *Agoraphobia* is the fear of open spaces. Actually it is much more than that. It is the terror of having another uncontrollable panic attack, especially in public. This type of phobia can keep women from ever leaving their homes.

2. Discuss the differences between specific/special phobias and social phobias; between agoraphobia and specific/special and social phobias.

3. Read Proverbs 3:21-26 and take turns answering the following questions:

    a. Define "sound judgment" and "discernment" as used in this text. What is the practical significance of each? Why are they essential to life? (see vv. 21-24).

    b. What does the writer of Proverbs tell you concerning feeling fear of sudden disaster? (v. 25).

    c. Why should you, as God's daughter, be unafraid in life? (v. 26).

    d. When do you experience your greatest amount of panic-fear? How can you overcome it with the advice Proverbs 3 gives?

Group Prayer to Pray: *Lord, please help us deal with our unhealthy fears that cause us distress and discouragement, and that interfere with our daily activities. Help us recognize those irrational fears other people experience so that we might know how to reach out to them with wisdom and knowledge and prayer. And help us and others to know that nothing can separate the Christian believer from your always-present love and care. In Jesus' name we pray, amen.*

Section 4: Face Your Fears

Ask your group of women to read Chapters 16-20. Meet together, and participate in the Group Bible Study:

1. Briefly share a highlight from Chapters 16-20 that particularly spoke to you.

2. Taking turns, read aloud Hebrews 11:1-40. Discuss the fifteen people Paul named as having the faith needed to face their fear and respond courageously to God's challenge. Can you identify with the fears and faith of any of these people? Why? How?

3. What other Bible character comes to mind when you think of extraordinary faith in the face of fear? Share his or her story and the strength you gain from the scriptural account.

4. (Only if you feel comfortable doing this in front of the group:) Name a time in your personal life when a hardship caused you fear, and God gave you needed strength to face and conquer it. How do you think depending on God's presence, loving care, deliverance, strength, and peace can help you deal with future hardships?

5. (Again, only if you feel comfortable doing this in front of the group:) Name a time you faced a loss that broke your heart and crushed your spirit. Did you find that God provided the comfort you needed at the time of your loss? If so, explain.

6. Read Psalm 34:17-18 aloud in unison: "The righteous cry out, and the Lord hears them; he delivers them from all their troubles. The Lord is close to the brokenhearted and saves those who are crushed in spirit."

7. Spend a few minutes as a group memorizing this passage, taking it a phrase at a time. What a great promise to meditate on whenever you feel anxious or worried.

Group Prayer to Pray: *Lord, we pray that you will help us to "be still and know" during the days we struggle with our fears. Please provide us with your comfort during our hard times. Help us not to worry about the threat of future losses. We pray also for all the world's women who face bereavement of any kind. O Lord, we know of no woman who has not, in some dark hour, faced the fear of loss. We pray that women experiencing loss and pain and discomfort will turn to you, and seek your presence and reassurance. In Jesus' name we together pray, amen.*

SECTION 5: Conquer Your Fears with Christ's Example

Ask your group of women to read Chapters 21-25. Meet together, and participate in the Group Bible Study:

1. Briefly share a highlight from chapters 21-25 that particularly spoke to you.

2. Take turns as a group reading John 1:1-18. Then discuss the following question: How did "the Word became flesh" influence and/or impact your life?

3. If you wish to, describe to the group your conversion experience, and tell how it changed your life.

4. Read aloud the following questions. Take a couple of minutes to ponder them and respond as you feel led.

   a. Do you fear death and dying because you worry about your salvation, and where you will spend eternity? (If you answered yes, please explain.)

   b. Do you fear death and dying because you worry about the welfare of loved ones you leave behind? (If you answered yes, name those loved ones and describe why you worry about them.)

   c. Do you fear death and dying because you are frightened by the actual process of dying and the suffering it might include? (If you answered yes, explain what you are afraid of: possible pain, suffering from accident, devastation from disease, another's cruelty? Tell why.)

   d. Think back to the story of Lazarus, including the imaginary conversation we had with him after Jesus raised him from the dead. Discuss any new insight you gained about death from this "angle" on the story.

Group Prayer to Pray: *Father, the thought of suffering and dying scares me. I cannot control the time or place or method I will depart this world. It is a mystery to me. I fear the pain and suffering it may cause. I fear for the welfare of those who depend on me. But, Lord, I am sure of where I will spend eternity. You have promised your children that you have prepared a place for them to live forever. I am willing to face the suffering and uncertainty of death, Lord, because it will bring me Home to you. I pray, Lord, that you will teach me to accept suffering like Jesus did. In Jesus' name I pray, amen.*

SECTION 6: Testimonies of Fears Conquered

Ask your group of women to read Chapters 26-30. Meet together, and participate in the Group Bible Study:

1. Briefly share a highlight from the chapters (26-30) you read. What particularly spoke to you?

2. Paul speaks often about courage in the face of fear. Paul listens to Jesus, and to God's angel, takes their advice to be strong, and passes that encouragement to others who face terror and persecution. Read each Scripture listed below and discuss as a group each particular verse's words of wisdom, especially as it relates to women today:

   a. Acts 23:1: Paul stands condemned to possible death before the Sanhedrin.

   b. Acts 27:24: Paul sails for Rome and encounters a storm at sea.

   c. Phil. 1:14: Paul, in prison, writes to the Philippians.

    d.   2 Tim. 1:7: Paul tells Timothy....

    e.   Phil. 4:13: Paul confesses....

3. Read more about Paul's extensive sufferings in 2 Corinthians 11:16-33. What attributes do you see in Paul's life that you'd most like to have in your own life? Explain why.

4. After reading this book, what new insights have you gleaned on the topic of fear and how to deal with it from a biblical perspective? Share a story, if you'd like, of how God is helping you overcome your fears.

<u>Group Prayer to Pray</u>: *Father, we see how, throughout the ages, ordinary people like Paul and Timothy, Perpetua, and Felicitas have been called to live extraordinary lives and suffer excruciating deaths. We pray for the kind of courage each of these heroes shows when faced with terrifying situations and the nearness of death. Give us their strength. Help us to face our own fears, Father, and, with your help, to conquer them. In your name we pray together, amen.*

SCRIPTURAL PRAYERS TO PRAY
WHEN YOU (OR A LOVED ONE) FACE
PAINFUL SITUATIONS

Praying Scripture is one of the "most powerful things we can do to dissolve our fears and to grow in our relationship with the Lord."[1]

I pray that the following Scripture verses will comfort you in your times of fear and distress.

Scriptures to Pray:

When you *feel anxious*, pray: "Lord, I will cast all my anxiety on you because you care for me." (1 Pet. 5:7)

When you *feel frightened*, pray: "Lord, when I feel fear and trembling, when my heart is in anguish within me, when horror has overwhelmed me, when I want to fly away and find peace, show me how to cast my cares on you. For you have promised to sustain me." (Ps. 55:4-8, 22)

---

[1]   Cheri Fuller, *Fearless* (Grand Rapids: Fleming H. Revell, 2003), p. 34.

When you *feel timid*, pray: "Lord, your Word tells me that you did not give me the spirit of timidity, but the spirit of power, of love, and of self-discipline. Help me, Lord, to receive my strength from you." (2 Tim. 1:7)

When you *feel discontent*, pray: "Lord, when in my season of life I feel discontent, help me to realize that there is a time for everything, and a season for every activity under heaven: a time to be born and a time to die, a time to plant and a time to uproot. I pray, Lord, for your contentment. Free me from my restlessness. Increase my faith. Give me new purpose." (Eccles. 3:1-2)

When you feel *lonely*, pray: "Lord, thank you for your reassuring words: 'Never will I leave you; never will I forsake you.'" (Heb. 13:5)

When you feel *confused* pray: "Lord, please let me feel your presence when I am confused and frightened. Help me to know that you are always before me, and I will not be shaken." (Ps. 16:8)

When you feel *weak*, pray: "Lord, I give my weakness to you. Your Word tells me that 'I can do everything through him who gives me strength.' I pray for that strength. Go before me, Lord, and fight for me when my enemies seek to hurt me. Help me not to be fainthearted or afraid. Help me not to be terrified or to give way to panic." (Phil. 4:13; Deut. 20:3-4).

When you feel *isolated*, pray: "Lord, just as Moses told Joshua many years ago, may I too take these words to my heart and no longer feel isolated: 'The Lord himself goes before you and will be with you; he will never leave you nor forsake you. Do not be afraid; do not be discouraged.'" (Deut. 31:8).

When you feel *unloved*, pray: "Lord, I am convinced that neither death nor life, neither angels nor demons, neither the present nor the future, nor any powers, neither height nor depth, nor anything else in all creation, will be able to separate me from your love that is in Christ Jesus my Lord." (Rom. 838-39).

When you face *violence*, pray: "Lord, help me not to be afraid of those who can kill my body but cannot kill my soul." (Matt. 10:28).

When you face *tragedy*, pray: "Lord, in this world I know I will face trouble. Help me to face it unafraid. For I can rest in the knowledge that you have overcome the world." (John 16:33).

When you face *hardship*, pray: "Lord, thank you for your words regarding faith for the times I face hardship and need encouragement. You tell me, 'Righteousness from God comes through faith in Jesus Christ to all who believe,' (Rom. 3:22) 'Faith is being sure of what we hope for and certain of what we do not see.' (Heb. 11:1) 'We have been justified through faith,' and 'we have peace with God through our Lord Jesus Christ, through whom we have gained access by faith into this grace in which we now stand.' (Rom. 5:1-2) Help me, Lord, to live by faith, not by sight." (2 Cor. 5:7).

When you face *phobias*, pray: "Lord, I cry out to you and you hear me. You deliver me from all my troubles, my fears, my phobias. Thank you for being close to me, for

I am brokenhearted and crushed in spirit. Teach me to give my fears to you and be released from my phobias." (Ps. 34:17-18).

When you face *fear*, pray: "Lord, where can I go from your Spirit? Where can I flee from your presence? If I go up to the heavens, you are there; if I make my bed in the depths, you are there. If I rise on the wings of the dawn, if I settle on the far side of the sea, even there your hand will guide me, you right hand will hold me fast." (Ps. 139:7-10).

When you face *panic*, pray: "Lord, thank you for the peace you give me. It is unlike what the world can give me. Keep my heart from feeling troubled. Help me not to panic. Be close to me when I am afraid. Thank you, Lord, for your wonderful peace." (John 14:27).

When you face *cruelty*, pray: "the Lord is my helper; I will not be afraid. What can man do to me?" (Heb. 13:6). "In my anguish I cried to the Lord, and he answered by setting me free. The Lord is with me; I will not be afraid. What can man do to me? The Lord is with me; he is my helper. I will look in triumph on my enemies." (Ps. 118:5-7).

When you face *hatred*, pray: "Lord, help me to love my enemies, and to pray for those who persecute me." (Matt. 5:44-45).

When you face *surgery*, pray: "Lord, please let me not be anxious about anything, but in everything, by prayer and petition, with thanksgiving, present my requests to God. Let me know your peace, which transcends all understanding. Peace that will guard my heart and mind in Christ Jesus." (Phil. 4:6-7).

When you face *disease*, pray: "When I am afraid, I will trust in you. In God, whose word I praise, in God I trust; I will not be afraid." (Ps. 56:3).

When you face *accident*, pray: "Lord, you will cover me with your feathers, and under your wings I will find refuge; your faithfulness will be my shield and rampart. I will not fear the terror of night, nor the arrow that flies by day, nor the pestilence that stalks in the darkness, nor the plague that destroys at midday." (Ps. 91:4).

When you face *overwhelming trials*, pray: "Lord, you tell me that you are my helper. I will believe you, and I will not be afraid." (Heb. 13:6).

When you face *trouble*, pray: "Lord, you have promised me your peace—that sense of deep contentment even when I face this world's difficulties. I will not let my heart be troubled. I will not be afraid. I will simply trust you." (John 14:27).

When you face *harm*, pray: "Lord, you promise to keep me from all harm, to watch over me as I go about life—in my coming and going, now and always." (Ps. 121:7-8).

When you face *natural disasters*, pray: "Lord, you created me, and you formed me. You tell me not to fear because you have redeemed me. You have called me by name and I belong to you. Lord, I will not fear when I pass through deep waters, for you will be with me. I will not be afraid when I pass through swift rivers, for you will keep them from sweeping over me. I will not be afraid when I walk through life's fire. You will keep me safe and unburned.

I will be afraid of nothing nature can do to me, for you are always with me." (Isa. 43:1-5).

When you lack *peace*, pray: "I take your words to heart, Lord, when I lack peace. Thank you for telling me: 'Peace I leave with you; my peace I give you.… Do not let your hearts be troubled and do not be afraid.'" (John 14:27).

When you face *lack of trust*, pray: "Lord, you are my refuge and my fortress. I will trust in you. I will rest in your shadow and in your shelter. Almighty God, Most High." (Ps. 91:1-2).

When you face *dying*, pray: "Lord, even though I walk through the valley of the shadow of death, I will fear no evil, for I know that you are with me; your rod and your staff, they comfort me." (Ps. 23:4).

When you face *lack of faith*, pray: "Lord, thank you that I have been justified through faith in you. Please instill within me that peace that your faith brings. I want to live by faith, and not be deterred by the frightening events that happen around me. I want to stand strong in faith and not be afraid." (Rom. 3:22; Heb. 11:1; Rom. 5:1-2; 2 Cor. 5:7).

When you fear *dying*, pray: "Lord, you say that in your Father's house are many rooms. That if it were not so, you would have told me. You offer me assurance, Lord, when you tell me that you are going there to prepare a place for me and my loved ones. And that if you go and prepare a place for me, you will come back and take me to be with you that I also may be where you are. You assure me that I know the way to the place where you are going. (John 14:1-4). Thank you, Lord.

When you fear *death*, pray: "Lord, I have been crucified with you, and I no longer live. You live in me. I live by faith in you, Jesus, because you gave yourself for me. I do not fear death. You have overcome death." (Gal. 2:20).

When you fear the *Evil One*, pray: "Lord, help me to stand firm in my faith and resist the Evil One." (1 Pet. 5:9). "Lord, protect me from the Evil One." (John 17:15). "Lord, thank you for your promise when you tell me: 'You, dear children, are from God and have overcome them [the Evil One and his demons], because the One [God] who is in you is greater than the one [Satan] who is in the world.'" (1 John 4:4).

When you fear *losing your way*, pray: "Lord, thank you for your words that show me the way to you. You tell me that you are the way and the truth and the life. That no one comes to the Father except through you." (John 14:6).

When you fear *aging*, pray: "Lord, when I grow old, help me to know that youth and beauty are temporary, but what I do for you is eternal. Help me to dismiss the fear of losing my youth. Help me instead to proclaim with Paul: 'I have fought the good fight. I have finished the race, I have kept the faith.' For that is what really counts in this life, Lord." (2 Tim. 4:7).

When you fear *fear*, pray: "You, Lord, are my refuge and strength, my ever present help in trouble. Therefore I will not fear, though the earth give way and the mountains fall into the heart of the sea, though its waters roar and foam and the mountains quake with their surging." (Ps. 46:1-3).

When you need *comfort*, pray: "Lord, no matter where I go, your Spirit goes with me. Even if I wanted to, I could not hide from your care. As high as heaven and as low as Hades, you are with me. You are with me day and night. You comfort me when I travel, no matter where I go. I trust you will always guide me and keep me safe in your hand." (Ps. 139:7-10).

When you need *courage*, pray: "Lord, you stay center-stage in my life, always in my thoughts. I will not be afraid. I will not be anxious. You give me courage to face life and not tremble." (Ps. 16:8).

When you need *faith's affirmation*, pray: "Lord, you've promised me that if I have faith as small as a mustard seed, I can move mountains, and I can uproot mulberry trees and plant them in the sea. Lord, please increase my faith!" (Matt. 17:20; Luke 17:6).

When you need *hope*, pray: "thank you, God, that you so loved me that you gave your one and only Son, that if I believe in him, I shall not perish but have eternal life. Please help me to share this word of everlasting hope with others who need hope." (John 3:16).

When you need *support and companionship*, pray: "Lord, you are my faithful companion, 'my hiding place.' You will protect me from trouble and surround me with 'songs of deliverance.' (Ps. 32:7). You are my shelter, my refuge, and my fortress. My God, I will trust in you completely." (Ps. 91:1-2).

When you *lose a loved one*, pray: "Lord, death has been swallowed up in victory. When I lose a loved one to death, I can ask death: 'Where, O death, is your victory? Where, O death, is your sting?' (1 Cor. 15:55; Isa. 25:8; Hos. 13:14).

I know, Lord, that one day you will wipe every tear from our eyes. And there will be no more death or mourning or crying or pain." (Rev. 21:4).

When you *are hurting*, pray: "Lord, thank you for your Holy Spirit—the Counselor, the Spirit of Truth. Thank you that I know him—that he lives with me and in me. Thank you, Jesus, for your eternal promise: 'Because I live, you also will live.'" (John 14:16-17, 19).

When you are *discouraged*, pray: "Lord, you are the vine, and I am the branch. I will remain in you, and I will bear fruit. For apart from you I can do nothing." (John 15:5).

A List of Common Phobias[1]

Acrophobia: fear of heights

Agoraphobia: fear of open spaces

Arachnophobia: fear of spiders

Atychiphobia: fear of failure

Aviophobia: fear of flying

Bathophobia: fear of depth

Carcinophobia: fear of cancer

Ceraunophobia: fear of thunder

Claustrophobia: fear of confined spaces

Enochlophobia: fear of crowds

Gerascophobia: fear of growing old

Rhytiphobia: fear of getting wrinkles

Glossophobia: fear of speaking in public

Hydrophobia: fear of water

Limnophobia: fear of lakes

1   From Time.com, "Phobias from A to Z," compiled by Fredd Culbertson, August 2, 2003.

Thalassophobia: fear of the sea

Iatrophobia: fear of doctors

Katagelophobia: fear of ridicule

Lygophobia: fear of darkness

Metathesiophobia: fear of changes

Misophobia: fear of dirt or germs

Verminophobia: fear of germs

Necrophobia: fear of death

Thanatophobia: fear of death or dying

Ophidiophobia: fear of snakes

Pyrophobia: fear of fire

Sciophobia: fear of shadows

Taphephobia: fear of being buried alive

Testophobia: fear of taking tests

Triskaidekaphobia: fear of the number 13

Xenophobia: fear of strangers

About the Author

Denise speaks around the world to women's groups, churches, colleges, and seminaries. She teaches "The Writing Minister: How to Write to Publish" to seminarians and pastors at Beeson Divinity School, Samford University, Birmingham, AL. She is married to Dr Timothy George, founding dean of Beeson Divinity School. They are parents of two grown and wonderful children: Christian Timothy George, and Alyce Elizabeth George; and one delightful daughter-in-law (Christian's wife) Rebecca Pounds George.

Denise George is author of more than two dozen books, including: *While the World Watched* (Tyndale House Publishers, 2011, by Carolyn McKinstry with Denise George); *I Am My Sister's Keeper* (Christian Focus, 2011); *Johnny Cornflakes: A Story About Loving the Unloved* (Christian Focus, 2010); *The Secret Holocaust Diaries: The Untold Story of Nonna Bannister* (Tyndale House Publishers, 2009); *What Pastors Wish Church Members Knew* (Zondervan, 2009); *What Women Wish Pastors Knew* (Zondervan, 2008).

Other titles from Christian Focus: *God's Gentle Whisper: Developing a Responsive Heart to God* (2007); *Our Dear Child: Letters to your baby on the way* (co-written with her husband, Timothy George, 2006) and *Teach Your Children to Pray* (2004).

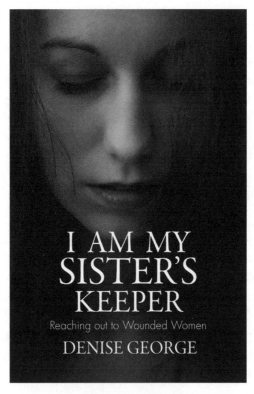

I AM MY SISTER'S KEEPER

Reaching out to Wounded Women

DENISE GEORGE

ISBN 978-1-84550-717-6

I Am My Sister's Keeper
Reaching Out to Wounded Women

Denise George

And just as Jesus compassionately loved those who were suffering, so can we. 'As Christian women, our hearts ache with a world that suffers,' author Denise George cries. 'Our love for God compels us to put our love into action.'

I Am My Sister's Keeper tenderly addresses issues like broken relationships and divorce; unforgiveness; loneliness; spouse abuse; and loss and grief. Through biblical stories and contemporary stories of wounded women, George's advice guides readers in how to pray, offer a listening ear, share from their own experiences and encourage others with God's promises. A complete Bible study guide makes this an ideal resource for groups of women to study together.

With the love of Jesus poured out through his followers, hurting women begin to overcome painful circumstances. Through our hearts and our hands, God still heals wounded women.

I found I Am My Sister's Keeper *a genuinely Christian response to particular issues that cause much suffering among many women in today's world. It motivated me to care more deeply for women I meet by sensitively listening to their stories, praying for and with them, showing practical love, and especially by sharing God's love for them in Jesus.*

Moya Woodhouse
Faculty wife at Moore College
Sydney, Australia

Christian Focus Publications

Our mission statement –

STAYING FAITHFUL
In dependence upon God we seek to impact the world through literature faithful to His infallible Word, the Bible. Our aim is to ensure that the Lord Jesus Christ is presented as the only hope to obtain forgiveness of sin, live a useful life and look forward to heaven with Him.

Our Books are published in four imprints:

CHRISTIAN FOCUS

popular works including biographies, commentaries, basic doctrine and Christian living.

CHRISTIAN HERITAGE

books representing some of the best material from the rich heritage of the church.

MENTOR

books written at a level suitable for Bible College and seminary students, pastors, and other serious readers. The imprint includes commentaries, doctrinal studies, examination of current issues and church history.

CF4•K

children's books for quality Bible teaching and for all age groups: Sunday school curriculum, puzzle and activity books; personal and family devotional titles, biographies and inspirational stories – Because you are never too young to know Jesus!

Christian Focus Publications Ltd,
Geanies House, Fearn, Ross-shire,
IV20 1TW, Scotland, United Kingdom.
www.christianfocus.com